why baseball matters

yale

university

press

new haven

and

london

susan

jacoby

why

baseball

matters

Published with assistance from the Mary Cady Tew Memorial Fund.

Yale University Press books may be purchased in quantity for educational, business, or promotional use. For information, please e-mail sales.press@yale.edu (U.S. office) or sales@yaleup.co.uk (U.K. office).

Set in Times Roman and Adobe Garamond types by Integrated Publishing Solutions.

Printed in the United States of America.

Library of Congress Control Number: 2017952550
ISBN 978-0-300-22427-6 (hardcover : alk. paper)

A catalogue record for this book is available from the British Library.

This paper meets the requirements of ANSI/NISO Z39.48-1992 (Permanence of Paper).

10 9 8 7 6 5 4 3 2 1

also by susan jacoby

Strange Gods: A Secular History of Conversion
The Great Agnostic: Robert Ingersoll and American
 Freethought
Never Say Die: The Myth and Marketing of the
 New Old Age
Alger Hiss and the Battle for History
The Age of American Unreason
Freethinkers: A History of American Secularism
Half-Jew: A Daughter's Search for Her Family's
 Buried Past
Wild Justice: The Evolution of Revenge
The Possible She
Inside Soviet Schools
Moscow Conversations

In memory of my grandparents
James L. Broderick and Min Broderick

It seems to me that through baseball I was put in touch with a more humane and tender brand of patriotism, lyrical rather than martial or righteous in spirit, and without the reek of saintly zeal, a patriotism that could not so easily be sloganized, or contained in a high-sounding formula to which you had to pledge something vague but all-encompassing called your "allegiance."

—Philip Roth, "My Baseball Years"

contents

introduction

Never make predictions, especially about the future.

—CASEY STENGEL

Early one Sunday morning in the spring of 1987, I was awakened
by a phone call and heard a booming voice ask, "Is this Miss
Susan Jacoby?" "Who is this?" I inquired suspiciously. "This is
Ernie Banks," he replied cheerfully. "Oh, right," I said and was
about to hang up when he cut in, "I'm calling from Chicago to
thank you for mentioning me in your wonderful review of Gary
Carter's book today in the *Tribune*." Then I realized that the
caller might actually be Banks, the beloved All-Star shortstop
for the Chicago Cubs when I was growing up in the 1950s. I
had indeed written a review for the *Chicago Tribune* of a baseball
book titled *A Dream Season,* by Carter, the starting catcher for
the 1986 world champion New York Mets. Carter had begun his
book with the simple sentence, "I keep thinking about Ernie

Banks."[1] He went on to mention Banks as one of the many great players—elected to the Baseball Hall of Fame in his first year of eligibility—who never got a chance to participate in a World Series. Banks spent his entire nineteen-year career with the then-woeful Cubs, in the days when a player had no right to switch teams without the assent of his owner. Because my review was to be published in Chicago, I naturally picked up Carter's allusion to Banks in my opening paragraph. Reverting to the voice of an awed ten-year-old, I said tentatively, "This is really . . . Mr. Banks." "Call me Ernie," he replied. "Call me Susan," I said. We went on to have a long talk about the two great Chicago shortstops of the 1950s—Banks and Luis Aparicio, who played for my team, the White Sox. It all came back to me—the sun-swept afternoons at beautiful Wrigley Field, home of the Cubs, and ugly Comiskey Park, home of the Sox. Banks's iconic baseball plea, "Let's play two," on a fine day when one nine-inning game didn't seem to be enough. Aparicio's dazzling footwork in the field. The recollected happiness of a game that has been a part of me for nearly as long as I can remember—a game I learned in front of the television set in my grandfather's bar. Concluding our conversation, Banks gave me the greatest compliment any baseball legend could give a mere fan: "I told myself when I read that article, 'The girl is *in the game.*'"

I became a passionate fan because my grandfather owned a bar and bowling alley in Harvey, Illinois, a blue-collar community just south of Chicago. Until I was ten years old, I spent the better part of my summer Saturday afternoons knocking back Shirley Temples while Gramps's customers explained the inside game to the little girl sitting on a bar stool with her legs propped up by liquor cartons. My grandfather had invested shrewdly in the first color television set in the neighborhood. (He had invested just as shrewdly in 1932, two days after Franklin D. Roosevelt won the Democratic nomination for the presidency, in a decrepit bar that had been shuttered throughout Prohibition. "Everyone knew that Roosevelt was going to win," he told me, "and that it was just a matter of time until beer would be legal and then everything else. I was terrified that someone would snap this place up in the forty-eight hours it took me to round up $100—no easy task, I can tell you—for an option to buy as soon as I could get a lawyer to draw up the papers." (Prohibition, which had been in effect since January 17, 1920, was repealed on December 5, 1933.)

As South Siders, nearly all of my grandfather's customers were Sox fans, although we occasionally watched the Cubs (especially if the still-Brooklyn Dodgers were in town and we would get a chance to see Jackie Robinson). By the time I was in first or second grade, I was very much aware of the significance of Robinson. In the summer of 1953, Gramps took me to Wrigley Field because the Dodgers were in town. Jackie didn't do anything special that day, but every time he stepped up to the plate, he was greeted by a combined chorus of cheers and boos, with taunts of "nigger" audible among the latter. (Banks, who would become the first black player for the Cubs, was not on the field. He was called up from the minor leagues in September, and his first full major league season was 1954. I am told by Cubs fans of my generation that racial epithets vanished rapidly from Wrigley after Banks, who became one of the most popular players in the club's history, established himself as that rare baseball figure, a power-hitting shortstop.) During the game I attended with my grandfather, I was very upset. The word "nigger," which I had heard on the school playground, was explicitly forbidden in both my parents' and my grandparents' homes. Gramps turned around and told one man in the row behind us to stop using such language in front of children, but the day was spoiled. I couldn't stop talking about it at the bar the following Saturday, and one of the men said to Gramps, "Jim, you shouldn't have exposed her to that." He replied, "She should grow up knowing what other people have endured." Then he added—I remember this precisely—"I'm ashamed of myself that I didn't say something a lot stronger."

Ah, those long, talk-filled Saturday afternoons, ending only when (if the game didn't go into extra innings) wives came to fetch their husbands home for dinner around 5 o'clock. There was nothing I wanted to do more than listen, on and on, to the arguments—about baseball and everything else—conducted in Chicago's distinct second- and third-generation Irish American accents. I now realize that this regular time out of time, spent listening to and talking with adults while watching the game we all loved for as long as the game lasted, was as different from today's technology-obsessed childhood as my childhood was from the one described by Laura Ingalls Wilder in her *Little House on the Prairie* series, set in the 1870s and 1880s. Looking back, I see that when I walked into my grandfather's bar, I was not only getting ready to watch the White Sox play the hated Yankees but was entering the previous seven decades of American history, as taught by the men who, like Gramps, had been born in the late 1880s and 1890s.

I told a young friend—a fantasy baseball enthusiast who rarely attends games or watches them on television—that I was planning to write a short book about the challenges facing baseball, as a game and a business, in an era of fragmented attention spans and unprecedented competition for fans' attention among all sports. His response was, "Oh, you're going to write another one of those books about how wonderful things would be if baseball remained exactly the same as it was twenty or thirty years ago—sunny afternoon games, the green of the field, fathers playing catch with sons . . ." That is not my intention, because I do not think that everything about the game was better several decades ago—or even in the halcyon days preserved in selective memories of my childhood. (Actually, sunny afternoon games had become as rare by the late 1980s as players who spent their entire careers on one team.) My concerns about the future of baseball—a $10 billion sport enjoying an unprecedented era of financial success and labor peace—are not based on misplaced nostalgia for a "pure" game that never existed. They are based on the dissonance between a game that demands and depends on concentration, time, and memory and a twenty-first-century culture that routinely disrupts all three with its vast menu of digital distractions.

To regain the attention of young fans, baseball will have to reinvent itself again—as it did after the First World War, when the lively-ball era came into its own with the arrival of Babe Ruth;

as it did when the old system of a team "owning" players was replaced by free agency in the late 1970s; as it did when baseball finally owned up to its drug problem, which vitiated so many records of the 1990s.

Can baseball get the minds of the young back in the game, even though the culture of my grandfather's bar is gone? I hope so, because next to reading and making love, no other pastime has given me more pleasure and knowledge throughout my life. But I never make predictions, especially about the future.

I

the good

and bad

old days

The best words, the most fun words in our language are "Play ball."

—FORMER COMMISSIONER OF BASEBALL PETER UEBERROTH

Before baseball can move ahead to confront the true challenges posed by the twenty-first century's culture of distraction, it is necessary to distinguish between essential memories of the real game and an unwarranted idealization and mythicization of a pastime often presented as part of an age of innocence that never existed. When I hear older fans talk about this so-called innocence, I am always reminded of what one of my father's contemporaries, a World War II combat veteran, said about the tendency of Americans to call the battle against the Nazis "the good war"—in contrast to the controversial "bad war" in Vietnam. "There are just wars," my dad's friend said, "but no war should ever be called good."

I suspect that my own nostalgia, to the extent that it colors my thinking about baseball, has as much to do with the grandfather I loved, and with his bar, as with the game itself. But there is certainly nothing warm and fuzzy about the memory of racial epithets spouted in a major league ballpark six years after Jackie Robinson became the first black American to play in the twentieth-century major leagues. Indeed, this experience belonged to the decidedly unsentimental side of my education, in a school more realistic and rigorous than the one I attended on weekdays.

Baseball, the business, is and always has been affected and afflicted by all the social realities of American life—from racial segregation through drug use. But if the business of baseball is just like life, the game of baseball, as it is played on the field, is anything but a reflection or representation of ordinary experience. Those of us who love the game between the lines should acknowledge that we love it precisely because it is *not* like life. Baseball, played as it should be, is fair and governed by rules. Never was the difference between baseball and life demonstrated more vividly, in a fashion that could be backed up by statistics as well as emotion, than during the thrilling 2016 World Series between the Chicago Cubs and the Cleveland Indians—a seven-game drama with a final act that ended during the closing weeks of the most disturbing and mendacious presidential campaign in modern American history. Was the presidential election "rigged," as then-candidate Donald J. Trump claimed? (Presumably it was not, since Trump won in the electoral college—while losing the popular vote—even though he had insisted that the proceedings were rigged against *him*.) But the millions of Americans, Trump and Hillary Clinton supporters alike, who forsook the endless campaign coverage for the World Series could be certain of one thing: the spectacle they were watching on the field wasn't rigged—right through the dramatic ten-inning comeback win by the Cubs in the seventh game. According to Nielsen Sports, more than forty million Americans tuned in to the decisive contest, making it the most-watched baseball game in twenty-five years. It may not be surprising that in Chicago and Cleveland, 70 and 69 percent of households with television sets on were tuned to the game. (This figure is known as a "share" in the ratings industry.) What is more surprising is that throughout the country, in places with no rooting interest in either team, the share was 40 percent.[1] Viewership for the seventh game of the 2017 World Series, in which the Houston Astros defeated the Los Angeles Dodgers, was down 28 percent from the 2016 seventh game. The lower ratings were due not to any lack of excitement in the overall seven-game series but to a more pedestrian final game, in which the Astros took command with five runs in the first two innings.

In both 2016 and 2017—years marked by political upheavals and natural disasters—a lifelong baseball fan could be reasonably certain of one thing: the men on the field were playing by the rules, and most of the rules would have been just as recognizable to my grandfather as they are to me. Yet for any modern fan who looks at baseball honestly, nostalgia cannot be the driving force in love of the game.

Yes, I plead guilty to a wistful longing for more of the day games I remember from my childhood, but the truth is that during the week, like most adults, I can make time only to watch night games. I still hate the American League's designated hitter rule, adopted in 1973, which eliminates a key strategic element from the game—the manager's decision about when or whether to remove a pitcher in favor of a pinch hitter. And I am not happy about the game's current tilt toward strikeouts and home runs (both of which have been occurring at a record rate in recent years).[2] I realize that there are many fans who can't get enough of home runs, but I am already sick of seeing too many games in which sluggers hit the ball out of the park with no one on base but seem unable to bring a runner home from third with less than two out by hitting an undramatic fly ball or single. I state these reservations up front in the interest of truth-in-packaging. Fans like me, according to one writer who favors speeding up the game, have "grouchy" reasons for resisting any proposed changes in baseball. Grouchy reasons such as "the sanctity of the record books" and "the game's intergenerational history." Grouchy reasons that amount to "tired pieties that hold progress at bay."[3] But is it grouchy to insist on distinguishing between changes for the better and changes for the worse? Baseball, despite its robustness as a business, faces a number of serious challenges that guarantee change in the next decade. The question is which changes will enhance rather than detract from the special national significance and beauty of the game.

Indeed, part of the reason I love baseball as much as I did when I was a child is the game's periodic ability to reinvent itself and transcend some of its self-inflicted abominations as well as external social pressures.

When I was a child, back in the "good old days," Major League Baseball (M.L.B.) operated with a so-called reserve clause in the uniform contract that prevented a player from negotiating for what his services were worth on the open market and bound him to one team for his playing life—unless his owner agreed to trade him (or, as also happened, traded him against his will). Baseball as it was then, however famous and beloved some of its stars became, resembled nothing so much as indentured servitude. This truth was not fully understood by the many American men who fantasized about the privilege of being a serf in Wrigley Field or Yankee

Stadium. They seldom considered how they would feel if, when offered an ordinary job by an employer at a higher salary, they could not accept because their present "owner" had exclusive rights to their services. I heard almost no talk about the economics of baseball when I was learning the game as a child. My grandfather did mention Babe Ruth's famous response, when, in 1930, a reporter asked him whether he thought he ought to be making $80,000 a year when President Herbert Hoover's salary was only $75,000. "I had a better year than Hoover," the Babe supposedly said.[4]

The reserve clause was hardest on great players like Ernie Banks, whom no owner in his right mind would have traded in the prime of his career. Mediocre players, by contrast, sometimes had the good fortune to be traded and land on a winning team. The reserve clause was finally abolished in 1975 after years of bitter dispute, culminating in a lockout of players by owners who refused to accept an arbitrator's ruling—upheld by the courts—against them. Although the owners had predicted that the end of the reserve clause would mean the end of baseball as a business, that did not (surprise, surprise!) happen.[5] Eventually, the owners and the players' union reached an agreement, modified many times over the years, in which any player can become a "free agent," and negotiate with any team, after six years in the major leagues. Yet even today there are curmudgeons who fulminate about the vast riches a great, or even an average, player can acquire under the current system. This sentiment is probably the reason why Marvin Miller, head of the players' union between 1966 and 1982—the bitter height of the battle over the reserve clause—has, shamefully, not been admitted to the Baseball Hall of Fame.

I am not among the curmudgeons. Why shouldn't players with extraordinary skills—skills that, as baseball statistics tell us clearly, decline for nearly everyone after the early thirties—make what they are worth to their teams in the days of their youth? I don't begrudge Gary Carter or Reggie Jackson the money they made or the money I spent on tickets to see them play. (Jackson, who signed a five-year, $2.96 million contract with George Steinbrenner's New York Yankees in 1976, was among the early free agents who were able to take advantage of the reserve clause's demise. One of the most frequent comments from older fans at the time was that no one playing "a kid's game" was worth that much money—which didn't stop the grumblers from watching Jackson's epic home runs.) Why would I, as a fan, feel nostalgic for the days when the player who provided the thrills called his employer his owner? The brilliant pitcher Tom Seaver—the face of the young Mets franchise and its transformative leader from lovable losers into 1969 world champions—was traded to the Cincinnati Reds in 1977 after M. Donald Grant, the Mets' chairman of the board, told him, "You're making too much money at a young age. It isn't good for you."* As Seaver explained to the writer Roger Angell, "My owner said that to me. And for me to say 'my owner' is the most ridiculous thing in the world. Does anybody *own* anybody

---

*Seaver had signed a three-year contract in 1974—a year before the abolition of the reserve clause—paying him $225,000 a year. The salary was much lower than that commanded by the best of the new free-agent class—Reggie Jackson being a prime example. When Grant refused to renegotiate his contract, Seaver agreed to a trade (and the Cincinnati Reds agreed to pay him far more).

else in this country?"[6] There is a strong case to be made that if baseball had not reinvented its business model, with the players pushing the owners every step of the way, the preindustrial character of the game's labor relations would eventually have poisoned the well for many fans as well as the players themselves.

To cite a smaller example of baseball's capacity for reinvention —or for correcting its own mistakes—one need only turn to the 1980s, the heyday of artificial turf—surely one of the greatest atrocities produced by late-twentieth-century technology's application to sports. Fake turf is now a bad chapter in baseball history, in part because its unyielding surface was responsible for many player injuries. When it came time to build new parks to replace the artificial turf stadiums dating from the 1970s, the green of the field was, once again, made of grass. The 1992 opening of Oriole Park at Camden Yards in Baltimore, the first of the new grassy "retro" parks, was part of a process of self-correction at which baseball seems, albeit often grudgingly, to excel.

Of course, putting sod back on the playing field is much easier than facing and correcting a moral flaw that undermines the perception of baseball's fairness—the heart of the game's enduring appeal. The steroid era of the late 1990s and early 2000s, which casts doubt on every record set during that period, was just such a moral flaw, and it vitiates the marketing of nostalgia to fans over age twenty. Both players and owners initially preferred to turn a blind eye to what was happening. In 2007, a report submitted to the commissioner of baseball by former senator George Mitchell of Maine concluded that for more than ten years, there had been "widespread use of anabolic steroids and other performance enhancing substances by players . . . in violation of federal law and federal policy," and that those "who have illegally used these substances range from players whose major league careers were brief to potential members of the Baseball Hall of Fame."[7] (Mitchell, who was knighted by Queen Elizabeth II in 1998 after helping broker a peace agreement in Northern Ireland, was a man whose judgment and impeccable negotiating credentials could not be dismissed.) He had plenty of hard evidence for his report, because in 2002, M.L.B. and the players' union had signed the first random-drug-testing agreement for players. In 2005, disgusted fans had listened as their former athletic idols did their best to evade the questions of a congressional investigating committee. For most viewers, the evasions came across as outright lies—though they were clever lies that did not meet a legal definition of perjury. Given the public's general disapproval of Congress's performance, expressed in repeated public opinion polls, it ought to be difficult for any witness at a legislative hearing to appear insolent rather than sympathetic. Nevertheless, the former slugger Mark McGwire managed it. His mantra throughout the 2005 hearings was "I'm not here to talk about the past." What fan, after hearing that, could feel like anything but a dupe for having taken great pleasure in the 1998 contest between McGwire and Sammy Sosa in pursuit of Roger Maris's record of 61 home runs in a single season? (McGwire wound up with 70 homers and Sosa with 66.) Sosa, who also testified before the committee, was more measured in his language. "To be clear, I have never taken illegal performance-enhancing drugs," he said. That sounds clear enough, were it not for the fact that over-the-counter anabolic steroids are legal in Sosa's native Dominican Republic, where he spent much of the off-season. One of the saddest cases was Rafael Palmeiro, who flatly denied using steroids but tested positive for the anabolic steroid stanozolol just two months later—as he was closing in on his 3,000th hit. Palmeiro, one of only five players in baseball history to have ended his career with more than 3,000 hits and 500 home runs, would surely have been elected to the Hall of Fame had he not been entangled in the steroid mess. Moreover—unlike some other high-profile players involved in the investigations—he was always considered a model teammate and a model of community service off the field. Nearly all the players who were engulfed by the steroid scandal, including Barry Bonds and Roger Clemens, would probably have been great had they never used banned performance-enhancing drugs to extend their careers, heal from injuries more swiftly, and bulk up their muscles—thereby pursuing an advantage over those who played by baseball's traditional rules. It should be noted here that because baseball had no drug-testing policy in the 1990s, these players are guilty only in the court of baseball opinion, as reflected in the Mitchell report. In real criminal proceedings, Clemens was acquitted of federal perjury charges in 2012, and Bonds's conviction for obstruction of justice was overturned by a federal appeals court. (Human growth hormone, which Clemens was accused of using, is much more difficult than anabolic steroids to detect in urine.)

The history of the steroid era remains highly contested today, since many star players from the 1990s have been (so far) barred from enshrinement in Cooperstown. That may change, because younger members of the Baseball Writers' Association (the group that selects Hall of Fame members) tend to judge players like Clemens and Bonds less harshly than their older colleagues for having set records while juiced up on banned performance-enhancing drugs. On this issue, I hope that the older heads prevail. I consider it entirely possible, though, that future generations of sportswriters, raised in a culture far more permissive regarding many types of drugs than was the case as recently as the 1980s, will decide that the statute of limitations has expired and let the ancient steroid users into the Hall of Fame. (One of the stupidest arguments for granting the drug abusers a pass is the frequently proffered rationale that players like Babe Ruth were known to drink heavily and there is no reason why they should be in the Hall of Fame while Bonds and McGwire are kept out. This argument ignores the fact that alcohol, unlike steroids and human growth hormone, is a performance-impairing rather than a performance-enhancing drug—on and off the field.)

The real importance of the Mitchell report, with its account of a pervasive drug culture within baseball, lies in its application to the spirit as well as the letter of rules designed to establish an equal playing field.

No one has articulated the significance of rules more precisely, albeit in a different context, than A. Bartlett Giamatti, best known as a classics scholar and the president of Yale before he became president of the National League in 1986 and commissioner of Major League Baseball in 1989. Giamatti was interpreting baseball's rules against players gambling on the game, but the same logic would later apply to stars who had set records while using banned drugs.

In Giamatti's final act as commissioner—his time in office lasted only five months because he died of a heart attack at age fifty-one—he banned Pete Rose from the game for life because he bet on baseball as a player and a manager. The commissioner's statement combined idealism with tough-mindedness, and it upheld a standard of fairness somewhat higher than the measures of fairness, insofar as they exist, are applied to life outside the lines.

> I believe baseball is a beautiful and exciting game, loved by millions —I among them—and I believe baseball is an important, enduring American institution. . . . It will come as no surprise that like any institution composed of human beings, this institution will not always fulfill its highest aspirations. I know of no earthly institution that does. But this one, because it is so much a part of our history as a people and because it has such a purchase on our national soul, has an obligation to the people for whom it is played—to its fans and well-wishers—to strive for excellence in all things and promote the highest ideals.
>
> I will be told that I am an idealist. I hope so. I will continue to locate ideals I hold for myself and my country in the national game as well as in other of our national institutions. And while there will be debate and dissent about this or that or another occurrence on or off the field, and while the game's nobler parts will always be enmeshed in the human frailties of those who, whatever their role, have the stewardship of this game, let there be no doubt or dissent about or goals for baseball or our dedication to it. Nor about our vigilance and vigor—and patience—in protecting the game from blemishes or stain or disgrace.
>
> The matter of Mr. Rose is now closed. It will be debated and discussed. Let no one think that it did not hurt baseball. The hurt

will pass, however, as the great glory of the game asserts itself and a resilient institution goes forward. Let it also be clear that no individual is superior to the game.[8]

That last sentence illustrates to perfection why the game of baseball (as distinct from the business of baseball) is quite unlike American life. To Rose's defenders, who consider it a travesty that baseball's all-time hit leader (at 4,256) is not in the Hall of Fame, every word in Giamatti's statement condemns him as an unreasonable prig. But Giamatti was not a prig, if one accepts the various dictionary definitions that define priggishness as a self-righteous moralism that assumes superiority to others. Giamatti's conclusion that no individual is superior to the game is surely one he would have applied to any person involved in baseball—including himself. Baseball must not only be fair; it must be seen to be fair—even, or especially, when its finest players are involved. That is all Giamatti was saying. That is all, and that is more than enough.

I like to imagine, had Giamatti lived long enough to leave his mark on the game as a strong commissioner, that he might have done more than his successors to head off the era of steroid abuse. But I also doubt that a sophisticated man who took as much pleasure in the action on the baseball diamond as he did in the gems of Renaissance art and literature, would have given up on the game because it didn't comport precisely with his childhood memories. So what if I would prefer that the Cubs, as well as all other teams, play more of their games in sunlight? Could anything have been more exciting, during the day or night, than the team winning its first World Series since 1908 after falling behind three games to one in 2016? Could anything have been more uplifting, in the final weeks of a campaign fueled by resentment of the Other, to see our oldest national game being played at the highest level by people of various races, nationalities, and ethnicities?

Baseball is a game—a beautiful and admirable game that originated in a particular part of the North American continent, the United States of America, for a crazy quilt of reasons that have never been pinned down by legions of obsessed sports historians. That, too, is enough. Make baseball more than an engrossing, difficult, stimulating, and beautiful game, and you set yourself up for bitterness and disappointment.

Consider the case of the cultural historian Jacques Barzun, whose 1954 observation "Whoever wants to know the heart and mind of America had better learn baseball" is probably the most widely quoted encomium to a sport ever written by an intellectual.[9] Not so widely quoted are Barzun's more hyperbolic descriptions of the game at the midpoint of the twentieth century, among them "Happy is the man in the bleachers. He is enjoying the spectacle that the gods on Olympus contrived only with difficulty when they sent Helen to Troy and picked their teams."[10] But things didn't work out well in Troy—not, at least, for the humans on the divinely chosen teams. Barzun went on to describe baseball as "the true realm of clear ideas"—a game unlike any known in Europe. "That baseball fitly expresses the powers of the nation's mind and body," Barzun added, "is a merit separate from the glory of being the most active, agile, varied, articulate, and brainy of all group games."[11]

It cannot be emphasized enough that the French-born Barzun was writing at the height of American power in the American century, at a time when baseball managed the neat trick of representing the values of a more pastoral, often mythical American past as well as the promise of a better, different kind of future—embodied most visibly by the entry of black Americans into the major leagues. Barzun's analysis of baseball was a tribute not only to a sport but to the unifying American cultural values the sport represented (or so it was thought at the time). As we now know, the 1950s marked the beginning of the end of a period when the vast majority of Americans believed in the existence of a homogeneous culture. The fragility and exclusionary nature of many supposedly unifying values would not begin to manifest themselves forcefully until the late 1960s. It may not be surprising, though it is saddening, that a man who had compared the fans in the bleachers to the gods might be embittered when, by the end of the century, ballparks seemed to have acquired elements (for example, exploding scoreboards, ear-shattering music) more reminiscent of Hades than of Olympus. Barzun, who died in 2007 just a few weeks short of his 106th birthday, had reportedly changed his mind about the game altogether by the early 1990s, when he was quoted by many sources to the effect that he had become "so disgusted with baseball, I don't follow it anymore."* The commercialization of the game, he charged, was "beyond anything we ever thought, the overvaluing, really, of the game

*I am fudging this attribution because, although the quote appears in many articles by sportswriters and on many baseball Web sites, none of the references explain under exactly what circumstances Barzun was supposed to have renounced baseball and all its works. His comment is always said to have been made in 1993.

itself. It's out of proportion to the place an entertainment ought to have."[12] Well, yes. But comparing baseball to the Trojan War and the enjoyment of bleacher creatures to the gods on Olympus did not exactly place the game within the ordinary realm of entertainment either.

I can understand the depth and timing of Barzun's disappointment in the business of baseball. The second half of the 1990s ushered in the steroid era, but the first half produced the greedy expansion that established three divisions in each league, thereby ensuring a third lucrative round of playoffs. More often than not, the ensuing wild-card playoffs send at least one genuinely mediocre team to a "postseason" that, in the northern states, often threatens to run into the first November snowdrops. The three-tier playoff system began in 1995. It was supposed to start a year earlier, but the entire 1994 postseason was wiped out as the result of a prolonged labor battle. The cancellation of the 1994 World Series enraged fans of all ages and revived the old resentment about player salaries. Indeed, the unwillingness of many in baseball to confront steroid use could be traced, in part, to the fact that juiced-up sluggers and home run derbies had brought fans back to the ballpark after the labor strife that characterized the first half of the decade.

Nevertheless, baseball—the beautiful but decidedly non-Olympian pastime—not only did penance for its sins but, through some tortuous labor negotiations, figured out a way to transcend them and discourage (though not rule out) repetition of the same follies. Pharmacological criminals have a tremendous financial incentive to develop and distribute new, undetectable drugs, and some players have shown that they will still take a chance on detectable drugs and hope that they don't get tested at an inopportune time. But that is the business of baseball, dealing with its problems exactly as other businesses do. The game on the field, however, has remained something more in tune with hopes that real life often dashes.

Baseball was first called "the national pastime" in print (insofar as scholars have been able to trace the history of the trillions of words written about the sport) by the *New York Mercury* on December 5, 1856. The game that would evolve into modern baseball, distinguished by the configuration of a diamond rather than a square or oval and the division of the playing field into fair and foul territory, was largely an urban and a New York–area pastime in the decade before the Civil War. *Porter's Spirit of the Times,* one of the earliest publications to provide extensive coverage of sports, described pre–Civil War baseball as "the National game in the region of the Manhattanese."[13] So much for the myth of baseball's pastoral origins—one of the many sentimental notions perpetrated and perpetuated throughout much of the twentieth century by gifted writers who ignored the fact that the first organized (though not professional) baseball teams outside Brooklyn and Manhattan appeared before the Civil War in such decidedly nonpastoral environs as St. Louis, Chicago, Milwaukee, Detroit, and Cleveland. Semiprofessional teams flourished in the decade after the war as industrialization and immigration swelled the population of cities in a legally (if not ethically or socially) reunited nation. Baseball was not yet an organized business; the better-known players were paid from unpredictable gate revenue and were in the position of insecure, albeit talented, freelance writers.

In 1869, Cincinnati's Red Stockings became the country's first openly professional team, touring the nation and providing season contracts for players.* Cincinnati was no more representative of a pastoral idyll than any of the other American cities with a lively baseball scene. Located in what was something of a gray area regarding attitudes toward slavery in the antebellum era (though Ohio was a nonslave state and fought for the Union), the border town became a boom town in the first decade after the Civil War.† In a sense, it was fitting that the first professional baseball team should emerge in a place on the cutting edge (almost literally) of a conflict that had come so close to destroying the American union. That conflict would, of course, continue to unfold within the segregated "national pastime" for more than eight decades.

In the second decade of the twenty-first century, the business of baseball has never looked healthier financially. Even before the blockbuster 2016 World Series, baseball pulled in annual revenues —from sponsorships, television contracts, and gate receipts—of more than $9 billion. Between 2015 and 2016 alone, money from sponsorships over the lifetime of contracts rose by 60 percent— from $225–250 million to $360–400 million.[14]

*The Red Stockings were not related to the current Cincinnati Reds, who date their continuous franchise, under slightly different names, from 1882.

†In southern Illinois and Indiana, there were similar patterns of ambivalence about slavery—especially when people had relatives on the other side of the Mason-Dixon line.

Yet it could be a mistake of Ruthian proportions to predict the financial fortunes of baseball on the basis of current revenues. Although baseball's dailiness is one of the main factors distinguishing "the national pastime" from other professional sports, interest in the game is also unusually susceptible both to the occasional spectacular World Series—and to a succession of dull seasons in which no one except fans of a particular team picks a favorite or cares who wins in the postseason.

In the late 1960s and early 1970s, for example, average attendance in ballparks was flat—around 15,000 fans per game.[15] But in 1975, the Boston Red Sox and the Cincinnati Reds played an extraordinary seven-game series, won by the Reds, that attracted large television audiences throughout the country. No one who was watching will ever forget the moment when the Boston catcher Carlton Fisk won the sixth game in the twelfth inning with a home run just inside the left-field foul pole. I can see, as if it were yesterday, Fisk gyrating toward fair territory with his entire body after he hit the ball—as if he still had any control over where the ball would land. The whole series, won by the Reds in the seventh game, mesmerized fans like me, who had no rooting interest in either team. The following year, baseball attendance topped 30 million for the first time in the history of the game. In 1977, average attendance was more than 18,000 per game—an increase of 20 percent from the pre-1975 figures.

The 1975 World Series was not the only force contributing to the cyclical revival of interest in baseball in the second half of the decade.

I turned thirty that year, and, like many people my age, my

interests had focused on the Vietnam War, the civil rights movement, and the beginning of the feminist movement throughout the sixties. I never completely lost interest in the game that was the love of my youth; when I was living in Moscow and beginning my first book in the summer of 1969, I would phone the American embassy regularly to find out the score of the most recent Mets game. But baseball was definitely on the back burner until I was caught up in the 1975 Series, which reminded me of everything about the game at its best.

I hadn't realized how much I missed it. For whatever reason, I returned to the ballpark to follow the Mets in person in 1976—just in time, as luck would have it, for the team to fall into a torpor under the stewardship of the owner foolish enough to let Seaver get away. And so it came to pass that the baseball gods would take their revenge in 1985, when Seaver won his 300th game in New York, where he was pitching for the Chicago White Sox against the Yankees in the Bronx. Oh, how I wished the milestone had been reached at Shea Stadium. What a wondrous thing it would have been to have Seaver on the rising 1985 Mets team to impart his pitching wisdom to the great young staff that included Dwight Gooden, Ron Darling, and Sid Fernandez. And how good it is to remember Seaver fighting hard for Number 300, at age forty, his face and physique the face and physique of a middle-aged man unenhanced by drugs—not throwing as hard as he did when he was young but winning with guile and grit.

But still, there is no real case to be made that baseball was much better way back when—because "when" means different things to fans of different putative golden ages. I prefer Seaver's way to Clemens's way, but that does not mean baseball was a more innocent game in the 1980s than it is today. Baseball's real challenges in this century lie elsewhere, in the way we use our minds rather than the other parts of our bodies.

The greatest problem baseball confronts in the twenty-first century is that it derives much of its enduring appeal from a style of play and adherence to tradition very much at odds with our current culture. In one sense, it seems ridiculous to speak about baseball as "challenged," given the profitability of the sport for both players and owners. But the demographic makeup of baseball's typical television audience delineates the challenge: it has the oldest, whitest fan base of any major sport.

If I weren't a woman, I would fit the typical fan profile perfectly. Nearly six out of ten fans for nationally televised baseball games are white men over fifty-five. Only one out of four people watching baseball on television is under thirty-five. Baseball also has fewer female and African-American fans than N.B.A. basketball, N.F.L. football or NASCAR. In only one respect does the baseball audience, whether at the ballparks or in front of television sets, resemble the changing demographics of American society: the game has a growing proportion of Hispanic-American fans—especially among the young. But many statistics show that young African Americans, like young whites, have been tuning out baseball in growing numbers. The greater presence of young Hispanic Americans in the fan base is undoubtedly attributable to the rising numbers of Latin American stars in major league baseball. For a variety of reasons, the proportion of black American players has dropped steadily since its high point in the 1980s. Most fans like to watch sports (all forms of entertainment, for that matter) in which they can see themselves in the game's brightest stars. If you're young, gifted, and black, you see more people who look like you playing in the N.B.A. than in M.L.B. If you're young, gifted, and Hispanic, baseball is the sport that permits you to see yourself on the field.

There is an aspirational quality about being a serious sports fan, even if you know deep down that you will never be good enough (if you are a kid) or would never have been good enough (if you are an adult) to play the game at the highest level. As a girl, I knew perfectly well that girls did not grow up to play big-league baseball, but that did not stop me from fantasizing about playing second base, like my hero Nellie Fox, for the White Sox. Fantasy is part of becoming a fan, even though the fantasy of becoming a major league baseball star must eventually be discarded by most men as well as women. That is not to say that someday a woman of extraordinary physical and athletic endowments might not reach the major leagues but that the odds against such a cometlike emergence are high. I would certainly like to be around to see the woman who breaks that glass ceiling (or green floor).

While gender, ethnicity, and race all affect baseball's fan base to one degree or another, I suspect that the aging of baseball's audience is largely attributable to the profound dissonance between a culture saturated with devices that offer instant gratification and a sport that requires intense, sustained concentration from its fans. Here I must acknowledge that every new technology has brought forth predictions about the death of baseball, often from shortsighted owners as well as from the sporting press. It seems almost incredible today to recall that both radio and television were initially viewed by many owners and sportswriters not as media that would expand the total audience for the game but as zero-sum competitors for ballpark attendance. Of course, one explanation for the animus of a large segment of the sporting press toward radio in the early 1920s was that announcers were becoming better known than newspaper sportswriters. One of my favorite quotes, from the *Sporting News* in 1925, warned that baseball "is more an inspiration to the brain through the eye than it is by the ear. . . . A nation that begins to take its sport by the ears will shortly adapt the white flag as its emblem, and the dove as its national bird."[16] (If there were a prize for mixed metaphors, this long-forgotten eruption would surely be a finalist.) In the late 1940s and early 1950s, television produced the same kind of anxiety about attendance from legendary baseball executives like Yankees General Manager Larry MacPhail (who tried and failed to prevent the sale of television rights to the 1947 World Series) and Dodgers President Branch Rickey. Eventually, of course—and sooner rather than later—all the clubs sold their television rights, and no one benefited more for decades than big-city teams.

Nevertheless, I must and do insist that the digital media are different. Listening to a game on radio or watching one on television demanded the same amount of time and attention as actually going to the ballpark. The difficulty of staying "in the game" in our culture of constant interruptions is responsible for the perception that nothing much is going on in sports that do not involve frequent scoring, as basketball does, or unpredictable shifts from defense to offense and vice versa. Neither radio nor television (with the exception of the small transistor radios that were used mainly on beaches and, surreptitiously, to check the score of World Series day games in school) was portable and therefore a transmitter of inattention.

In any ballpark, you can see (literally) the ways in which devices interfere with the focus required to appreciate the game unfolding on the field. Many fans under, roughly, age fifty—and nearly everyone under thirty—are scrolling continuously through their iPhone screens as play proceeds in front of them. When I first saw this phenomenon at Citi Field, home of the Mets, I thought the iPhone fans might be checking for a close-up of a play they had just seen. I soon realized that most of the people with heads buried in their phones were either texting or watching another sporting event altogether. (And there is almost always a competing sports event; as is well known, baseball now overlaps in September with football and in the spring with basketball and hockey.) Fans checking out another game on a screen can no more be "in the game" in front of them than drivers can operate an automobile safely while texting.

Baseball's vital moments, in comparison with most other sports', cannot be appreciated fully without an understanding of what has—or has not—happened before. (The home run is often an exception to this rule.) But when you watch a runner on third base beat a throw home for a run, it means very little if you were playing a video game on your iPhone while the player was staying out of a double play two batters earlier. Yes, you know that the runner scored—but you don't know exactly how and why he got to home plate. A dunk shot or a touchdown pass are much more dramatic in the moment, regardless of whether you understand what sort of bobbing and weaving or blocking and tackling made the scoring play possible. The perfect example of baseball's demand for concentration is the classic 1–0 pitchers' duel, which most novice fans find utterly boring. Most of the time, all that can be seen on the surface is hitter after hitter failing: making an out. Baseball executives have suggested in recent years that games are simply too long for many fans, but the real obstacle for many young fans may be the slow, sifting-and-sorting action within the game itself. Baseball is a game in which one must wait, pay attention, and wait again for startling, defining moments of action. Michael Haupert, a professor of economics at the University of Wisconsin–La Crosse who studies baseball as a business, puts it succinctly: "The problem for fans with a short attention span isn't the length of a baseball game, but the perception that nothing is happening within the game. Especially a low-scoring game."[17] Something *is* happening, of course: pitchers are consistently getting major league hitters out by throwing the ball where it cannot be hit solidly. But you have to understand a great deal about pitch selection and the art of hitting to comprehend the immense difficulty of what is going on in front of your eyes. You're not going to appreciate a shutout if you're standing in line for pizza, texting your friends, and only occasionally looking up at the huge television screen visible from the pizza line.

There are, however, many other powerful, less obvious forces affecting baseball—one of them being widening income inequality coupled with the high cost of an adult-controlled youth sports culture that did not exist when major league baseball was at the height of its popularity. Low-income parents, of whatever race, cannot afford the cost of the long training period and the travel that characterizes elite youth leagues—which serve as feeders for both high-level college baseball programs and the minor leagues.

The major predictor of whether anyone becomes a fan of any sport is whether a person played the sport as a child. But youth sports meant something much less structured and less elaborate when I was growing up than they do today; in fact, sports did mean playing instead of working. I played baseball in pickup games until I reached puberty (the age when active sports ended for nearly every girl who grew up in the prefeminist era). Playing softball at recess or in the vacant lot at the end of my block actually did help me learn the game, even though I had absolutely no athletic talent. One of the greatest memories of my childhood involves knocking in a run with a double in a game between the two fifth-grade classes in my school. It was the *only* hit I ever got. I knew I had hit the ball solidly (because for me, that was such an unusual feeling) and screamed at the runner on first to "go, go, go." Neither my utter lack of talent nor my gender prevented me from becoming a passionate fan, but I am not sure that would have been true had I never enjoyed the actual experience of playing pickup ball. Anything worth doing is worth doing badly.

That old saw would be anathema to anyone involved in the increasingly expensive and semiprofessionalized youth sports culture that has emerged during the past two decades in middle-class and upper-middle-class America. For athletically talented teenagers (in all sports, not only baseball), specialization is the name of the game. Baseball's complicated set of skills is now honed by private coaches and elite traveling youth leagues. In the hope of their child obtaining a college athletic scholarship, parents may spend thousands of dollars a year. Private coaching concentrates on power pitching and power hitting—the surest way to attract the attention of recruiters for the best-known college baseball programs and the minor leagues. One unexpected result: because fielding is given short shrift, many players who do obtain those coveted scholarships have to be taught how to throw the ball across the infield. At Tufts University, John Casey—a former president of the American Baseball Coaches Association —informs his players on the first day of practice: "You're no longer in the showcase world of display, display, display. We play baseball here—hit the cutoff man, do the little things that win games." He has also been known to further admonish the players that they have "been hitting off a tee in an indoor cage way too much. You could teach a chimpanzee smoking a cigarette to hit a baseball off a tee."[18]

Some researchers have concentrated not on income inequality but on the increase in single-parent households headed by women as the reason for the declining interest of teenagers, particularly African-American teenagers, in baseball. Until I began working on this book, I had no idea that there is an entire body of research (part of it academic, part conducted by the sports industry itself) suggesting that the single-mother home is the source of the problem. "We're looking at a generation who didn't play catch with their dads," says David Ogden, professor of communications at the University of Nebraska–Omaha and the author of a fifteen-year study of ten thousand youth baseball players. "Kids are just not being socialized into the game." The number of fatherless households among African Americans, Ogden suggests, is the main reason why the proportion of black players in the major leagues has fallen steadily during the past three decades.[19] Without those dads playing catch with their little boys, there is no natural pipeline into the big leagues. (This would strike me as a dubious proposition even if I didn't know that Jackie Robinson's father abandoned his family when Jackie was a baby.)

I do not doubt the validity of Ogden's statistics, but neither would I be surprised to learn that children from two-parent homes are more likely to be admitted to a top-notch university. Children raised by two parents have a great many advantages, period. Nor does Ogden's theory explain why teenage participation in all sports except soccer has dropped sharply since the turn of the millennium. Upper-middle-class parents, who spend a good deal of time shuttling their kids from one sporting competition to another, find this hard to believe. But the drop in youth sports participation is evident in every study of the subject and correlates not only with the rise of expensive elite training for promising high school students but with the increase in the amount of time teenagers spend on the Web. Correlation and causation are not, of course, identical, but the single mother as baseball killer seems to me a much less plausible hypothesis than either the cost of elite baseball training or the preoccupation of many teenagers with video games and social media. After all,

African Americans do learn to play basketball and grow up to become the largest group of players in the N.B.A. Is shooting hoops with fathers somehow less important than playing catch? While it is true that you can practice a jump shot by yourself but cannot catch a ball without someone to throw it to you, it is also true that getting a ball to fall through the hoop without defenders is extremely easy and teaches little about how to play basketball as a team sport.

My guess is that in two-parent as well as single-parent households, regardless of race or ethnicity, a child would have to be spectacularly talented—and the parents unusually sports-oriented—for a family to come up with several thousand dollars for special training on the slim hope that a teenager with a sweet swing will one day become a major league player. In spite of the natural desire to see children live out their dreams, most parents are not blind to the cruel trap that college athletic scholarships (in all sports) can pose for young people who will never make it to the pros—that is, for the vast majority of college players. The "student-athlete" who is given a pass on a research paper so that he or she can have more time for practice may wind up with a diploma and no job on or off a playing field.

In Latin America, the economic calculus for boys who focus on baseball in their early teens is completely different. The Dominican Republic, which has produced so many of the game's sparkling players since the 1960s (and where baseball has been popular since the last two decades of the nineteenth century) is a poor country with few job opportunities offering an escape from poverty. In 1983, Juan Marichal, who spent most of his career with the San Francisco Giants and won more games than any other major league pitcher during the 1960s, became the first Dominican-born player elected to the Hall of Fame. Pedro Martínez became the second Dominican elevated to Cooperstown in 2015. There are certain to be more Dominicans elected in the future. During the past three decades, M.L.B. has invested in youth leagues and first-class training for young Dominicans— and has been able to underwrite that training at a much lower cost than in the United States. Alan Klein, an historian of Latin American baseball, notes that the young hopefuls in the Dominican Republic have signed professional contracts but are not yet ready even for the rookie level of the minors in the United States. "The academies . . . offer the young players a world of plenty," Klein writes, "the likes of which they have never seen: as much food as they want, living conditions about which many could only have dreamed. They play with equipment that is second to none. With the material bonanza, however, comes a demand they not only comply as they never have before but also perform at ever increasing levels of baseball excellence. . . . They will be expected to learn new things and function in ways they cannot fully grasp to get to the United States, and no player gets to the United States without going through the academies."[20]

Under the leadership of Rob Manfred, commissioner since 2014, baseball is making a serious effort to bring more young African-American players back to the game—which would presumably attract more African-American fans. M.L.B. now operates a dozen urban academies in cities with predominantly black populations—programs that subsidize the elite level training that more affluent parents underwrite themselves. Such programs are not, of course, open only to African Americans, but they are concentrated in areas, like Compton, California, that used to produce more major league players at a time when expensive instruction for teens had not become a key element in player development. I have not been able to find any studies focusing on the proportion of current M.L.B. players born into poor white families, but it is reasonable to assume that working-class whites are no better able than working-class blacks to come up with the money for teenagers to spend their summers in traveling youth leagues instead of contributing to the family budget by working in fast-food restaurants.

The specialization of youth sports after middle school is the work of a society in which the culture of anyone playing catch with anyone seems as remote as the culture of my grandfather's bar. The umpire may still say "Play ball," but the message of adolescent specialization is "Work ball." Baseball is trying to address that problem too. In 2015, M.L.B. began a nationwide program called "Play Ball," which subsidizes informal baseball- and softball-related games like wiffle ball and stickball, for both boys and girls.

The inclusion of girls in these programs offers a nod to yet another of baseball's demographic problems—the relatively small presence of female fans. Many more women watch regular-season, nationally televised football than baseball (an average of 6.2 million versus 141,000 for each game day in 2015, according to Nielsen).[21]

Manfred, in an interview with me in the summer of 2016, emphasized that baseball remains the sport played by the largest number of children under twelve. "The real challenge is to keep kids interested after that, with all of the competition for their attention," he said. One of M.L.B.'s answers is its popular At Bat app, which, according to Manfred, is opened eight million times a day. The average age of users is under thirty. The question is whether snippets of games and baseball statistics are complementary to or competitive with the real thing. A few days after interviewing Manfred, I found myself in a New York City subway car next to a teenager who was using the At Bat app and wearing the cap of my beloved Mets. I asked if he had seen forty-three-year-old Bartolo Colón's outstanding 4–1 outing on the mound for the Mets the night before. He hadn't, he said, because he got bored when there was no scoring in the first three innings. He had, however, checked the final score before going to bed. This young man was certainly a fan—but a very different kind of fan from old folks who wouldn't dream of turning off a scoreless game after three innings. Obviously, anyone who uses the At Bat app, which enables viewers to access highlights from all major league games without actually watching an entire game, understands the mechanics and rules of baseball. And anyone who checks the score of his favorite team at night before going to bed has a rooting interest in the game. What this young man lacked was patience and the ability to concentrate at a time when balls weren't being hit out of the park. He wasn't interested enough to spend an hour (roughly the length of the three innings) watching Colón's fascinating and mysterious ability to control the movement of an 88-mile-per-hour fastball with the pressure of his fingertips. There was no scoring at the beginning and—this being baseball—there was no guarantee that there would be any scoring in the next three or six innings. Manfred sees the three-hour-plus length of the average baseball game as a major problem for young fans. But most proposals to shorten games (such as the silly elimination of actually throwing pitches to the plate for an intentional walk, which went into effect in 2017) shave only minutes off the game. It is difficult to make a case that my companion on the subway would have watched Colón's outing if the game had turned out to last two hours and forty-five minutes rather than three hours: both are unacceptable if you're looking for continuous action.*

Baseball is a game, to borrow a phrase from the writer Grace Paley, of "enormous changes at the last minute." The dramatic winning home run is less surprising if the hitter has been taking

---

*Colón won fifteen games—more than any other pitcher for the Mets in 2016. He was twenty years older than his nearest competitor, Noah Syndergaard, who won fourteen. Despite the pudgy middle-aged pitcher's winning ways and enormous popularity with fans, Mets management traded him to the Atlanta Braves, for whom he had a rocky start in 2017. In August, however, he turned up on the Minnesota Twins at age forty-four and became the oldest major league pitcher to throw a complete game since Jamie Moyer of the Phillies did it in 2010. After a standing ovation from the hometown crowd in Minneapolis—a familiar phenomenon for Colón—he said, "That was awesome." Whether he was referring to himself or the crowd was unclear.

"hard swings" throughout the game and "just missing the pitch," as sportscasters like to say.

It is counterintuitive to say that a sport can be an enormous financial success while losing the attention of younger fans who are the future of any sport—both as a business and as an American tradition. Yet it is difficult not to see trouble ahead in baseball's current television demographics. Nielsen, the arbiter of television ratings for generations, is now measuring viewing on mobile devices, but it is extremely difficult to determine how much of the game—as distinct from occasionally checking in—an individual is watching on an iPhone or iPad. Given what all of us, whatever our age, know about our truncated viewing habits on mobile platforms, it seems unlikely that the digitally distracted are watching a game with anything like the concentration of previous generations—whether raised on radio or on television. In theory, the ideal fan would be someone who watches some games on television and goes to the ballpark, if there is one within driving distance, several times a year. I am not talking about people who watch 162 games of a 162-game season. There is another name for this sort of fan—addict. Americans who plop themselves in front of the TV set and watch any sport for several hours *every* day are as addicted as those who spend hours on social media, playing video games, or engaging in "fantasy" sports on computers many hours a day.

The short and frequently interrupted concentration span of many Americans, so at odds with the traditions of baseball, is not a problem that can be solved in a direct, practical way—as the steroid crisis was dealt with through testing or the soulless artificial turf ballparks were fixed by laying down grass on new fields. Neither nostalgia for an innocence that never existed nor abandonment of the traditions that give the game its unique appeal will work. Those who own the game and play the game on the field must now face up to the tough job of thinking long-term in a society captivated by technologies that reward short-term thinking.

2 patience: a tale of two games

Baseball is essentially a 19th-century sport that is no longer congruent with American cultural dynamics and therefore seems slow and boring to many people.

—ARTHUR ASA BERGER,
Media Analysis Techniques

Anybody who knows the sport understands that the ninth inning is as valid as the first inning—that's why real fans always stay to the end of a game.

—ROY EISENHARDT,
FORMER PRESIDENT,
OAKLAND ATHLETICS

May 5, 2017, was a typical, slow baseball day and night for most of three-plus hours in Wrigley Field, where the Cubs met the Yankees, and at Citi Field in New York, where the Mets were playing the Miami Marlins. At Wrigley, where the afternoon game began at 1:20 p.m. Central Daylight Time, there were only two runs scored—by the Cubs—before the ninth inning. Boring nineteenth-century stuff, some might say. At Citi Field that night, the Mets found themselves down by six runs in the first half of the fourth inning. Although the Mets did score two runs in their half of the same inning, there was no more real action until the seventh inning. Boring. That is, if you are in sync with "American cultural dynamics," which assume the impossibility of waiting ten minutes, much less ninety minutes, for something to happen. Furthermore, whatever is happening must be so obvious that no prior knowledge of the subject is required. Arthur Berger, professor emeritus in broadcast and electronic communications arts at San Francisco State University, is quite right in his assertion—if, by cultural dynamics, one means the exaltation of inattention. (Here I cannot resist saying that communications arts—in spite of the fact that I am a graduate of the College of Communications Arts of Michigan State University—has always seemed to me a loathsome specimen of twentieth-century American academic jargon. With apologies to Georges Clemenceau, communications arts are to the arts as military music and justice are to music and justice.)

But, to give Berger his due, I certainly would not have been watching the afternoon Cubs-Yankees game on a twenty-first-century Friday had I not been confined to my apartment with a cracked kneecap. This provided both the opportunity and an extra incentive to watch a lot of baseball on that May day. The big nonsports news story, left over from the day before, was passage by the Republican-controlled House of Representatives of a health care bill aimed at repealing the Affordable Care Act (otherwise known as Obamacare). For nearly twenty-four hours, there had been dispiriting nonstop news coverage speculating about how many people with preexisting conditions would lose their health care if the bill ever became law, about higher premiums for Americans over fifty, about the loss of funding for contraception and abortion, about children who would lose Medicaid coverage. If escapism and fairness are partly responsible for the complicated appeal of sports, both seemed particularly appealing on such a day.

There is a nineteenth-centuryish feeling (or perhaps a general out-of-time feeling) attached to spending energy and attention on anything but work during the day. That (and the commercial revenue derived from the grasp of electronic communications arts on baseball and every other sport) is why M.L.B. plays nearly all of its games—too many—at night. There is no reason, apart from greed for more revenue from television commercials, for baseball to be played at night on Saturdays and Sundays. On the contrary: these are two days when most people can go to the ballpark and be reasonably certain of getting home at a reasonable hour, or watch a game on television without worrying about getting the kids to bed because tomorrow is a school day. To be fair, I must acknowledge that there are players who gripe about the heavy burden of having to play a day game after a night game, and there are some statistics to support the idea that teams fare worse on those days. To the griping players and the sabermetricians, I say: boohoo!

Although May 5 was a weekday, the Cubs-Yankees game took place in the afternoon because there are still many more day games played in Wrigley than in other major league ballparks. Wrigley, which opened as Weeghman Park in 1914, did not have lights for night games until 1988. The story of the political fight to bring lights to Wrigley makes for hilarious reading. Primarily because of objections by neighborhood residents who did not want their streets flooded by light from Wrigley (however much they liked being associated with this landmark), the Illinois General Assembly and Chicago City Council passed laws banning night games in Chicago. The legislation included a grandfather clause that exempted Comiskey Park, where the White Sox had been playing night games under lights since 1939.[1]

As it happened, both the Cubs-Yankees afternoon game and the evening Mets-Marlins contest offered near perfect illustrations of the combination of boredom and enormous changes at the last minute (or the last inning) that make the game so frustrating for those with a short attention span and so rewarding for the patient fan. "It takes a long time to understand baseball," says Michael Haupert. "One of the main reasons there's a slow learning curve is fairly obvious: the game is difficult, and failure is more common than success. If my students get a third of the answers right on their tests, they flunk. If a ballplayer gets a hit a third of the time, he's one of the high-level players in the game."[2] Glance at an N.B.A. game for more than ten seconds, and you're likely to see a ball fall through the hoop. Glance at a baseball game for the same amount of time, and you're more likely to see a foul ball or nothing at all, as the pitcher prepares for his windup or the hitter steps out of the batter's box.

As the first inning began at Wrigley, no one who grew up following baseball in Chicago would have been surprised to hear from the announcers what could be seen clearly on television—that the storied park, located less than a mile west of Lake Michigan, was a cave of the winds. Wrigley is a legendary hitters' park in midsummer, when the stifling Chicago heat and the wind blowing out toward the lake turn line-drive singles hitters into home run champions for a day. But in April and early May (and often in September), the wind holds up what would be sure home runs in July or August. The gusts blowing in off the lake also bedevil fielders, and routine pop-ups can become adventures that turn into runners who come around to score. It should be noted here that the wind at Wrigley—for both the home team and visitors—does not have a definitive impact over the course of an entire season. Mathematics geeks love to cite figures like a statistic indicating that 23 percent of the fly balls at Wrigley are deposited beyond the lush, ivy-covered center-field wall when the wind is blowing out, while only 13 percent leave the park when the wind is blowing in. But as David Kagan, professor of physics at California State University, notes, "the daily winds tend to cancel each other out over the course of a season."[3] The same would presumably be true of other cities with higher-than-average winds, which include New York, Milwaukee, San Francisco, Minneapolis, Cleveland, and somewhat surprisingly (to me), Kansas City. Wrigley presumably gets more attention because of its iconic status—comparable to that of Fenway Park in Boston—and because of Chicago's nickname, "the Windy City."

On this day in May, however, Wrigley would live up to every mile per hour of its reputation. With the wind blowing in at around twenty-five miles per hour—and gusts up to forty—plenty of normally harmless fly balls would be lost in the wind. And every run would be hard earned.

No one was expecting many, if any, home runs, but the Cubs deposited one in the right-field stands in their half of the first inning. The only other scoring, until the ninth inning, was a second Cubs line-drive homer to right field. Both homers were low enough and hit sharply enough—just in the right place—to avoid the full force of the wind blowing in from center field. Nothing much was happening, but the necessity to keep my knee propped up on a mound of ice focused my attention on fielding plays in the first and sixth innings that made the solo home runs more meaningful. In the Yankees' half of the first, the Cubs' Gold Glove right fielder Jason Heyward made a sliding catch of what looked like a sure sinking base hit by Yankee Starlin Castro. There was a Yankees runner straying from second base, and Heyward was able to throw him out easily for a double play. With the bases loaded and one out in the sixth inning, Heyward and the wind rescued the Cubs with yet another double play. Both home runs by the Cubs, in the first and sixth innings, followed outstanding plays in the field in the Yankees' half of the inning. (A good many fans believe that a stellar defensive inning is often followed by a stellar offensive inning, but there is little evidence in the ever-burgeoning world of baseball statistics to support this notion. What seems more likely is that difficult defensive plays are better remembered throughout the game if they were followed by an immediate burst of offense in the next half of the inning.)

For a fan paying attention, the game was never anything less than tense, given the thinness of a two-run lead and the lurking presence of a powerful Yankees offense. For fans who understand the inside game, there was another factor contributing to the suspense of inning after inning in which, to the uninformed, nothing much seemed to be happening. The Cubs would be unable to use their closer, Wade Davis, who had pitched in three straight games. Yet there was also the sense that the Cubs would probably win, given the obvious frustration of the Yankees at the windy conditions affecting so many plays. After the game, Yankees third baseman Chase Headley whined, "It was just a mess. It's really not baseball, to be perfectly honest. . . . The game's not close to what it's supposed to be played like. . . . I'm glad we don't have to play in those conditions very often because it just changes everything."[4]

I beg to differ. It absolutely is baseball—if by "it," one means variable weather conditions, park dimensions, and other unique features (such as the ivy-covered outfield wall at Wrigley) that affect both play on the field and the perceptions of fans. The weather, whatever it may bring, is part of the game. Headley is paid to play.* Baseball's playing conditions are not uniform—another factor distinguishing the game from many other professional sports, notably N.B.A. basketball and N.H.L. hockey.

Headley's comment was especially ungracious in view of the fact that the Yankees' change of fortune in the ninth inning—in which Headley himself played an important role—had nothing at all to do with the wind or the 45-degree temperature. With one out in the ninth, Headley nudged a single to left field. Then, with two out, pinch hitter Jacoby Ellsbury drew a walk. Two out, two on, with his team trailing 2–0, and the Yankees left fielder Brett Gardner stepped up to the plate. The second-best Cubs closer, the right-handed Héctor Rondón (remember, their best closer was unavailable), could not put away the left-handed Gardner. With the Yankees down to their last strike, Gardner caught a hanging slider and hit it 409 feet—a home run on any day, windy or not. In fact, the right-field wall at Wrigley is only 353 feet away from home plate. The result of the at-bat was not a total surprise, because Gardner had already seen six fastballs from Rondón. The hanging slider he finally hit over the fence must have looked very, very big. If there had been no one on

*I am using the term "paid to play" in its literal sense, not in the gross metaphorical sense in which the phrase is now used in political jargon.

base, the homer would have meant nothing. And neither Headley's nor Ellsbury's presence on base had anything to do with the wind. Yes, Chase Headley, that *is* baseball. It is a real pleasure to see a game in which players are required to summon up extra skill to battle nature as well as the opposing team. Final score: Yankees 3, Cubs 2.

On to the Mets-Marlins night game, which I probably would have watched even with a healthy knee. The Mets are my team. Nearly everyone in New York expected the Mets to cancel the game in advance. Heavy rain was predicted at some point in the evening, and the team's injury roster was already mounting and casting an ominous shadow over the rest of the season. For much of the night, Mets fans had every reason to wish that the game had been canceled.

The mood at Citi Field was grim before the game started, as the mediocre Rafael Montero took the mound in place of a badly injured Noah Syndergaard, known as Thor to the Mets faithful. With his flowing blond locks, the six-foot, six-inch pitcher did resemble a mythical image of a Norse god when he threw his best fastball up to 100 miles per hour. But the backstory to this game revealed that Syndergaard, who turned twenty-five in August 2017, was all too human—as are the baseball managers and executives who accede to the ridiculous notion that testosterone-fueled athletes in their early twenties are the best judges of how to maintain the health of their bodies. On May 1, Syndergaard had been placed on the disabled list after a magnetic resonance imagery test revealed a partial tear of his latissimus dorsi—a serious injury that would keep him on the disabled list for at least two months and, in a worst-case scenario, for the rest of the season. It is always a sickening sight to see a young athlete walk off the field in obvious pain; Syndergaard had left the mound, clutching his underarm, on April 30 in the second inning of what would turn into a 23–5 Mets loss to the Washington Nationals. The worst part of the story: Syndergaard had been complaining for at least a week about a sore biceps in his throwing arm, but he refused the request of Mets General Manager Sandy Alderson that he have an MRI at that point. Yes, a twenty-four-year-old baseball god who thinks he is immortal (as all twenty-four-year-olds—even those who cannot throw a fastball 100 miles per hour—tend to think) surely needs no advice from an older and wiser head about whether to undergo a noninvasive medical test that may tell him something he does not want to hear! Alderson's response was a classic: "I can't tie him down and throw him in the tube." True, and the contract between the Major League Baseball Players Association and M.L.B. also fails to require polio vaccinations or flu shots. But as one New York baseball writer wrote, it was clear "that Alderson should have been the grownup in this situation, [and] informed Syndergaard: 'It's the MRI tube or the disabled list. Take your choice.'"[5] Syndergaard might have wound up on the disabled list even if he had accepted the club's recommendation that he have an earlier MRI, but he would surely not have had the opportunity to sustain an injury so obviously painful that no one needed to be a doctor to recognize that horrible medical news was in the offing. Hence, Montero (with a 5.84 ERA as I write) took the mound on May 5. In three and two-thirds innings, Montero gave up five earned runs—and took ninety pitches to put his team at what looked like an insurmountable disadvantage. This was the sort of game you were certain your team was going to lose. In fact, I was paying very little attention by the fourth inning, when shortstop José Reyes failed to keep a soft dribbler in the infield—a mistake that led to six runs and chased Montero from the game. To add insult to injury, these were all two-out runs. In the Mets' half, center fielder Curtis Granderson hit a two-run homer that did not seem terribly important at the time but, in retrospect, kept his team in the game in spite of Montero's hapless performance.

During the game, I was reading an old essay about Bob Gibson, the great pitcher for the St. Louis Cardinals in the 1960s and 1970s, and I was wishing that Gibson could magically appear on the mound to rescue the Mets.[6] For those not old enough to have seen Gibson at work, one need only recall that 1968, one of the most tumultuous political years in American history, was known in baseball as "the Year of the Pitcher." Gibson had a record of 22–9 and an earned run average of 1.12—a combination milestone that will probably never be reached in the future because starters no longer pitch nine innings. (Whole books could be, and have been, written about this subject.)[7] Gibson's dominating record is often cited as the reason for M.L.B.'s decision to lower the mound in 1969.[8] There was, of course, no one resembling Gibson on the mound for either team on this night in 2017.

In spite of the fact that accounts of forty-year-old games seemed more interesting than the game before me, I did note that the Marlins failed to tack on runs in the fifth and sixth innings, when they had a runner on second with no one out and failed to score. The failure to "add on" when you already have a substantial lead is a cardinal sin in baseball, but you have to have watched a great many games, over a fair number of years, to understand this. After the game, Marlins manager Don Mattingly said, "You talk about adding on. The guys swung the bats well, but we let a couple of chances get away there late. Today, it came back to haunt us. You never know how many [runs] you're going to need."[9]

And so it came to pass that in the seventh inning, the Mets— down by only four runs instead of the six- or seven-run deficit they would have faced if the Marlins had added on those extra runs earlier in the game—came back with six straight hits to take an 8–7 lead. The star of the night was catcher T. J. Rivera, who hit a two-run double to tie the game. Wilmer Flores then walked home with the bases loaded for what turned out to be the winning run. Final score: Mets 8, Marlins 7.

Both baseball statistics and the ordinary experience of being a fan over a lifetime reveal how unusual it is for a team to come back from a four-run deficit after the sixth inning. According to an analysis of major league statistics encompassing all games played from 1957 through 2015, a visiting team going into the seventh inning with a four-run lead has a 95.08 percent chance of winning. Had the Marlins led by two more runs, the odds of their beating the Mets at Citi Field would have gone up to more than 98 percent.[10] Win expectancy calculations, provided by many analysts and used by millions of participants in fantasy sports, can vary considerably according to the variety of factors included. These specific statistics are based on average performance over a long period. They would obviously be somewhat different, for example, if one team had its best relief pitchers available while the other was forced to use the worst relievers in its bullpen. However, one need not be a sabermetrician to know that four-run comebacks late in the game are relatively rare. Roy Eisenhardt, the astute former owner of the Oakland Athletics, was right in theory but not in practice when he said the ninth inning matters as much as the first. If a team produces the unusual multiple-run comeback late in the game, of course the last inning matters as much as the first. But baseball is, as has often been said, a "game of firsts." A visiting team with a four-run lead in the first inning wins 83.44 percent of the time—which means that while the odds of a comeback are much better for the home team than they are if the visiting team maintains its lead into the seventh, they are still not good.[11] A statistic that may be even more surprising to all but the most dedicated fans tells us that in a majority of games, the winning team scores more runs in one inning than the losing team does in the entire game.

What keeps a true fan watching a seemingly lopsided game is not just hope but the memory of the unusual, thrilling comebacks that do occur. As many psychological studies have demonstrated, our personal memories are biased in favor of the unusual— including both good and bad events. In a fascinating study on nostalgic memories, one Boston University scholar notes that fans, "predicting their enjoyment of a football game they are about to watch . . . tend to recall the best game they can remember and base their predictions on their [recalled] enjoyment of that particularly good game."[12]

The same observation could surely be applied to baseball. I still recall in vivid detail every minute of the Mets' comeback against the Boston Red Sox in the tenth inning of the sixth game of the 1986 World Series. Losing by two runs, with no one on base, the Mets were down to their last out when Gary Carter nudged a single to left field. They tied the game not the way one would have expected—with a two-run homer—but in the most improbable way imaginable, with three consecutive singles and, as every Mets fan recalls, with a runner on third making it home after a wild pitch was dodged by the catlike Mookie Wilson. The Mets won after Wilson's ground ball found its way through the legs of the battered veteran Boston first baseman Bill Buckner, who was hobbled by two ankle surgeries dating from the middle of the 1970s. Sometimes when I am having an insomniac night, I put myself to sleep by replaying this half-inning. (Don't ask me why this works; I didn't get to sleep until 4 a.m. after the actual game.)

The rational part of me—the part that pays attention to statistics—doesn't believe for a minute that I will ever see a replay of such a gripping comeback. Like many games in the 1986 postseason, this one was, as a Mets pitcher (usually thought to be the eloquent Ron Darling) observed, simply "too fairy-tail-ish."[13] But that is why I remember it so well. After the game, some scribe went over his scorecard and discovered that there were thirteen two-strike pitches, most of them fouled off, that could have been turned into the last Mets strike and last out of the Series.[14] And that is why I watch and never quite accept that a game is hopeless—even though my own experience, as well as baseball statistics, tell me otherwise.

Rooting interest is the other vital, unquantifiable factor infusing sports memory. There is no real explanation for an adult's investment of emotion in what is—even the most besotted fan must admit this—essentially a commercial enterprise designed to separate the rooting public from as much money as possible. The abolition of the reserve clause, which denies most fans the pleasure of seeing a favorite player stick with one team for an entire career, has probably eroded fan loyalty to some extent—though fairness to the players is more important than stoking sentimentality based on servitude. For me, the one sorrowful note in the Cubs' shining 2016 World Series victory was the fact that Ernie Banks, "Mr. Cub," did not live to see it. No active player today is likely to be identified for decades, as Banks was both before and after his playing days, as the iconic representative of his team and his city.* "Mr. Met" is a mascot distinguished, appropriately enough, by his inflated baseball head. Yet I am a fan of the Mets, for reasons that do not bear too much logical scrutiny but are nonetheless real. First, I could never live in New York and root for the Yankees, because they were the fiercest enemies of my Chicago White Sox throughout the 1950s. Second, I am now a National League fan, because the league has resisted all appeals to adopt the designated-hitter rule. Third, my adult baseball memories are as firmly anchored in forty years

*Derek Jeter, who played his entire twenty-year career for the Yankees, may prove to be an exception. It's too soon to tell, because he retired from baseball only in 2014. Whether he will remain involved and identified with New York City, as Banks did with Chicago for the rest of his life, is an unanswerable question at this point.

of watching the Mets, in good times and bad, as my childhood memories are anchored in my grandfather's bar. That the Mets have not built as consistently excellent a franchise as the Yankees —that the former are not the best-known brand in American sports—is probably one of the reasons I love the team with the swell-headed mascot. Rooting for the Yankees is like rooting for JPMorgan Chase; the Mets feel more like my small neighborhood bank, which I still use for all routine financial transactions.

There is a bright, cherished thread of friendship and fun that binds baseball memory with rooting interest. Throughout the early 1980s, the Mets were rebuilding . . . slowly, slowly, in 1983 and 1984, then swiftly in 1985 with the emergence of young stars including Darryl Strawberry, Dwight Gooden, and Darling —and the experience of mature stars like Gary Carter and Keith Hernandez. I shared a season ticket with four people, and I looked forward to seeing them as much as I did to seeing Hernandez's perfect positioning at first base or "Doctor K" blowing away hitters before cocaine took its toll on his young career and life. And I didn't only like my fellow season ticket holders: I loved them in a fashion possible only when people share a secret virtue rather than a secret vice. We all knew that we could talk only to one another about our passion for baseball—that many of our nonbaseball friends could not comprehend how we could actually care about something that was, after all, just a game. There is nothing duller than being forced to hear a play-by-play account of a game belonging to a sport in which you have no interest—unless it is being forced to hear about a romance between two people you don't know.

In 1985—a year I remember with even more fondness than the championship 1986 season—fate placed me in London on a business trip when the Mets were playing the St. Louis Cardinals in a series, beginning October 1, that would determine whether the Mets had a chance to win the National League East championship. Since this was the era before personal computers, I woke up in my London hotel on October 2 not knowing whether the Mets had won the first essential game in St. Louis. The phone rang, and it was one of my fellow season ticket holders, who refused to reveal the outcome at the beginning of our conversation and teased me through ten innings of what had been a scoreless duel in St. Louis, in which Darling pitched the game of his life against the Cardinals' starter John Tudor. Only after a long, agonizing recap—beginning with Darling issuing an ominous walk to the leadoff hitter in the first inning—did my friend reveal that Strawberry, in the eleventh inning, had hit a line-drive home run with a hang time of only 1.5 seconds. The Mets' ace reliever Jesse Orosco stifled the Cards in the bottom of the inning, and the final score was 1–0. I whooped with joy and jumped up and down on the bed so vigorously that I spilled my morning tea on the Westbury Hotel's pristine sheets. That the Mets ultimately failed to win the league championship does not make the memory of that phone call less vivid or less pleasurable. Part of rooting interest is the special love of baseball friends who share irrational devotion to the same team—to the point of making transatlantic phone calls that, in 1985, were both expensive and the sole way of putting the absent baseball companion out of her misery in a chic quarter of London, so far from the Mets' anxious crowd.

Contrary to what many lukewarm baseball fans (and sports commentators) suggest, there is no one "right" way to watch a baseball game. Whether a fan is absorbing a game at the park, on television, or on a radio (the latter, these days, usually in a car), the current action coexists with what Roger Angell, in his classic 1972 book *The Summer Game,* called "the interior stadium." When the nineteen-year-old Gooden came up to the Mets in 1984, and began displaying the kind of control and fastball I had never seen in person, I began attending more games at Shea Stadium. It was possible then—before Gooden became a celebrity—to take the number 7 train out to Queens, walk up to the box office on game day, and, for less than $40, acquire an excellent seat in the mezzanine behind home plate. His nickname was "Doc," or "Doctor K," and enraptured fans put up a new "K" card in the corner every time he registered another strikeout. We all knew that we were seeing something special from this prodigy whose work combined the eagerness of an adorable puppy with an artist's image of a young god. The interior stadium, fortunately, does not allow its occupants to see the future. That year, I saw Gooden pitch in person several times and on television broadcasts many more times. Each had its advantages. On television, there was a close-up view of the pitcher's face and delivery that even the good seats in the park failed to deliver. At Shea, the interior stadium came into view in ways that it seldom did in my living room (or on radio, when commercial breaks are just as intrusive as they are on television).

I started thinking about Leroy "Satchel" Paige, the great pitcher who spent nearly all of his career in the Negro Leagues and who made his first major league baseball start, at age forty-two, for the Cleveland Indians in 1948. I was only three years old; of course I never saw him pitch. I thought about what it must have been like for a pitcher like Paige to have been deprived of the opportunity to display his full powers before American baseball's full audience. Even the most straightforward facts about Paige's life—like his age and birth date—were difficult to trace because of the invisibility of black Americans in many official records in the early 1900s. Larry Tye, author of Paige's definitive biography, notes that "in the post-Reconstruction Confederacy, it was easier to track the bloodline of a packhorse than of a Negro citizen."[15] Paige was born in Mobile, Alabama, in 1906, and descendants of slaves had not even been included in the Mobile census until 1902. Young Gooden, I thought frequently, would never be deprived of the attention that obscured the full achievements of older generations of African-American players —even the greatest of them. I wasn't at the ballpark, though, when I wrote a poem about this subject; I was watching Gooden pitch on television and took time during a commercial to dash off "To Dwight Gooden." I had just been thinking about Paige's frequently quoted admonition, "Don't look back. Something might may be gaining on you."[16] So I ended the poem with the lines "Tip your hat, Dr. K. / Nothing's gaining on you."

Although this is hardly a poem fit for anthologies of great English-language verse, it is an example of what goes on in the interior stadium regardless of whether one is paying attention in a ballpark, in front of the television set, or within range of a radio. I watched a great young black pitcher who seemed (before drugs entered the picture) destined for the Hall of Fame, and I began thinking about a black pitcher I had never seen—and whose race in Jim Crow America meant that there would be little archival footage of his performances for future fans. This interior dialogue between past and present, whether personal or social, is what goes on at times when nothing much seems to be happening, and that is why baseball cannot be appreciated fully by clicking on a tiny image on an app for two minutes.

The best writers about sports, like Angell, Frank Deford, Thomas Boswell, Daniel Okrent, and Wilfrid Sheed (to name only a few), used to be able to convey this interior dialogue. Today, even people who write about sports for a living have been infected by our impatient culture to the point where they often present baseball's great advantage as a liability. An unusually candid example of this genre is Jay Caspian Kang's confession in the *New York Times Magazine* that he had vowed to watch more baseball in the spring of 2017 because he was "trying to bring some routine to my life as a new father."[17] So far, so good. It sounds as if Kang was trying to do what I was doing in an attempt to assuage the pain of a cracked kneecap. Infants do have one thing in common with wounded knees: they require the caretaker to spend a good deal of time around the house. But then Kang found his attention flagging—much more, he said, than during a football or basketball game. He blamed his wandering attention, in part, on the "informational clutter" that pervades television broadcasts and leaves little room for the imagination. But wait. Kang went on to recall the "silent spaces in baseball that used to be filled in by novelists and filmmakers." Films like *Major League* (1989) and *Eight Men Out* (1988) "gave us thoughts of the batters as they dug into the box, the catcher's mantras and occasional trash talk, the umpire's endless exasperation. And while all that may have been a fantasy, it convinced you that what you couldn't hear or see while watching a baseball game could be translated directly into cornfed American English." Of course, Kang also references the 1989 movie *Field of Dreams,* in which an Iowa farmer, hearing voices murmuring, "If you build it, he will come," is impelled to construct a baseball diamond in his cornfield. "He" is Shoeless Joe Jackson, the most famous star involved in the 1919 Chicago Black Sox scandal. When the central character, Ray, does build his diamond, not only Shoeless Joe but the rest of the Black Sox turn up. The movie was based on the 1982 novel *Shoeless Joe,* by W. P. Kinsella, which also dealt with a son's troubled relationship with his dead father. *Field of Dreams* was a box office hit, but I really, really hated this movie. It bears the same relationship to baseball—a game played not by ghosts in the middle of farmland but by real people on real grass and dirt, mostly in the environs of real cities—as faux biblical movies of the 1950s, like *Ben-Hur* and *The Robe,* do to the birth of Christianity and real relations between Romans and Jews in first-century Palestine. What is truly awful, though, is a preference for movies that supply dialogue supposedly going on inside a pitcher's, a hitter's, or a fielder's head. That is what fans are supposed to supply in their interior stadium. The fun of watching a ballgame lies not in being supplied with scenarios by a screenwriter but in trying to figure out what the pitcher might be going to throw and why, and what the batter might be expecting and why.

Field of Dreams was not the worst movie of the 1980s in its dedication to sentimentality and unjustified nostalgia. That distinction goes to *The Natural,* the film adaptation of Bernard Malamud's 1952 novel. The novel is a bleak meditation on human talent undone by human psychological fallibility and on an America in which no achievement is ever quite enough (a work remarkably attuned to the class antagonisms that have helped fuel our current divisive politics). At the end of the book, the main character, Roy Hobbs, takes a payoff from gamblers to throw a critical game. In the movie, however, Hobbs affirms his own essential goodness (and, of course, the goodness of the game) by refusing the bribe and hitting a home run. Hobbs was played in the movie by the golden-haired, still young-looking forty-six-year-old Robert Redford, and that should have been the tipoff. If a director is looking for someone to cast as a brilliant athlete who betrays his talent, his sport, and, by extension, his country, he probably shouldn't be looking for someone whose physical presence, in youth and midlife, was the embodiment of everyone's image of an all-American.* The casting of Redford was all

---

*Redford was cast in the role of another kind of "natural" compromising himself in the 1972 movie *The Candidate,* which many critics consider one of the best political movies ever made. It could be argued that politics, then and now, is better suited than baseball as a cinematic background for a hero whose performance doesn't live up to either his outward appearance or his best ideals. In any case, Redford was the right age in 1972 to portray a young politician on the make.

wrong, precisely because he still looked so young and shining in 1982. The character of Hobbs, by contrast, is in his thirties and somewhat frayed around the edges. Picking an actor like Redford to play Hobbs was essential to the falseness of the movie: no one could imagine a player as adorable-looking as Redford throwing a game.

The 1980s—especially the latter half of the decade—were, as more than one scholar of baseball has observed, particularly well suited to smarmy nostalgia about the game. The older baby boomers, who came of age in the dissent-filled late 1960s and early 1970s, were settling into jobs and families. As Jules Tygiel notes, the adult fans of the 1980s were raised in the 1950s—"the last era in which professional baseball would reign as the nation's undisputed favorite sport."[18] Tygiel goes too far when he suggests that "many former protestors staged a symbolic homecoming through baseball."[19] There were a great many civil rights workers, antiwar protestors, and yes, feminists who never needed to stage a "symbolic" homecoming because they never left baseball in the first place. One important factor in the resurgence of interest in baseball in the late 1980s was that enough time had lapsed since the end of the reserve clause for boomers to get over their envy of the money being made by superstars (and even average baseball players). Many members of the boomer generation were doing well financially by the 1980s and were no longer shocked to hear that some guy playing a kid's game was making millions a year. That does not, however, explain the particular vulnerability to nostalgia embodied in so many of the films made about baseball in the closing years of the decade.*

Nostalgia is always a double-edged sword, whether the object is the history of the world or sports. In sports, the nostalgia engendered by baseball is particularly powerful because baseball has a more extensive statistical record and visual archive than any other sport. On the one hand, nostalgia for one's youth—the time when a child begins to understand the game and become a fan—is a powerful motivator for remaining or becoming a fan as an adult. On the other hand, nostalgia can become an aspiration in itself, as suggested by Kang's desire for cinematic dialogue to replace the game unfolding before him. This sentiment, from a new parent who knows a great deal about sports, demonstrates to perfection why baseball, in spite of its financial success, has a serious demographic problem. Numbers can lie, but the way people behave on a daily basis does not.

*For other views on this subject, see Michael L. Butterworth, *Baseball and Rhetorics of Purity: The National Pastime and American Identity during the War on Terror* (Tuscaloosa, Ala., 2010), and Vivian Sobchak, "Baseball in the Post-American Cinema, or Life in the Minor Leagues," in *Out of Bounds: Sports, Media, and the Politics of Identity,* ed. Aaron Baker and Todd Boyd (Bloomington, Ind., 1977).

3 who goes out to the ballgame and who doesn't?

If you miss your favorite N.F.L. team's game, you have to wait a week. In baseball, you wait a day.

—THOMAS BOSWELL,
Washington Post, 1987

I t cannot be said often enough that to predict the death of baseball because one young writer longs for movie dialogue to fill in the "silences" of a long at-bat would probably turn out to be every bit as silly as the 1925 prediction in the *Sporting News* that listening to baseball on radio was tantamount to waving a white flag of American cultural surrender. But the aging of baseball's audience—in a culture that requires no one to endure a waking moment without visual stimulation or noise—poses a unique demographic challenge that did not exist during the Roaring Twenties or in any predigital era. In 2015, according to Nielsen's annual year-in-sports report, approximately 59 percent of fans for national baseball television broadcasts were over fifty. Fewer than 47 percent of National Basketball Association fans fell into the same group.[1] In 2016, the estimated median age for all fans watching nationally televised baseball games was fifty-six.[2]

I am using the term "major," as it is generally used by the venerable rating firm Nielsen, to include M.L.B., the N.B.A., the National Football League, and the National Hockey League. Sports like golf, tennis, and soccer have ardent followings—soccer, in particular, has a growing male and female audience in the United States—but nevertheless reflect more specialized tastes than the four most broadly popular sports. An important caveat must be applied to consumption—and I use the word "consumption" deliberately—of all sports programming on all devices, ranging from traditional television to the newest iterations of the iPhone and iPad. The media landscape is changing so rapidly that direct year-to-year comparisons are difficult to make and would often be misleading. In 2017, Nielsen Sports released an analysis indicating that a staggering 78 percent of sports fans globally go online regularly while also watching sports on television.[3] Statistical breakdowns are not yet sophisticated enough to reveal whether these people are watching another sporting event online simultaneously, talking about the same game on Twitter or other social media, or doing something else entirely. Nielsen does estimate, however, that sports drive more than half of all conversations about television programs on Twitter.[4] This fragmented viewing pattern is bound to have a greater effect on baseball than on other major sports. I have stressed looking back on missed opportunities in the early innings as essential to making sense of later, more dramatic turning points. Any baseball game is a process, not a series of disjointed, disconnected events. The digital world is not about process but about instant delivery of results, so it is logical that younger viewers find it more difficult to focus on baseball than on faster-paced games like basketball, with its continuous action and frequent scoring.

The aging of baseball's audience is related to so many complex social forces outside the game that it requires a separate analysis transcending baseball's other demographic anomalies.[5] The graying of the fan base is also a sensitive subject with baseball people, many of whom refused to talk about the subject on the record. Few of the lords of baseball are as candid as Hal Steinbrenner, the Yankees' managing partner, who has acknowledged that one of the best-known franchises in any sport has had great difficulty attracting younger fans in recent years. "We recognized in looking at our fan base," he said, "we recognized in looking at our viewers on YES [the Yankees' local cable network], that that age group is not what it could be and not what it should be."[6] This remained true at the start of the 2017 season, despite the fact that the Yankees were off to a fast start, which provided a showcase for sparkling young players like catcher Gary Sánchez and outfielder Aaron Judge—a great baseball name if ever there was one. Inevitably, Yankees management swiftly designated an eighteen-seat section in the right-field stands—with a close-up view of Judge's position on the field—as "the Judge's chambers." Fans selected for the special seats deck themselves out in costumes designed to look like judicial robes. Just as inevitably, fans in the left-field stands—the sweet spot for any right-handed slugger in that ballpark—now call their own seats the Judge's chambers. If Judge continues to hit home runs as he did in his rookie season, there may be an entire stadium filled with fans in black robes.

Young people are as susceptible as older fans to baseball events that deliver special excitement. Buried in the gleeful reports by Fox Sports of record-setting audiences for the 2016 Cubs-Indians World Series was an increase among school-age viewers that outstripped the hefty increase among all fans. The average nightly audience increased by nearly 60 percent over the audience for the 2014 series, which also lasted seven games, between the San

Francisco Giants and the Kansas City Royals. But among boys from twelve to seventeen, the audience more than doubled.[7] This is a crucial demographic for the future of any sport, because real fans are almost always formed at some stage of childhood or adolescence. It remains to be seen whether the excitement of a high-tension World Series will carry over into future years and generate enthusiasm for more routine games. In 2015, viewers under seventeen made up only 6.8 percent of audiences for nationally televised games. It may be of even greater importance that viewers from ages eighteen to through thirty-four made up only 14.5 percent of the same audience.[8] That is why baseball's median age for national broadcasts is closer to sixty than fifty.

Of course, these figures do not answer the question of how many young people are watching baseball games, and how much of the games they watch, on mobile devices and through time-shifting technology that enables them to view as much or as little of a game whenever they want. Despite the increase in time shifting, Stephen Master, managing director for Nielsen Sports, says that the vast majority of athletic events are still viewed live. This conclusion reflects a decadelong trend. In 2015, sports accounted for 93 of the top 100 programs seen live on television—compared with only 14 of the top 100 in 2005.[9] The migration of quality television series to cable and streaming services may have a good deal to do with this change. A public accustomed to binge-watching dramas and tales of the supernatural still wants to see the outcome of real athletic competition in real time. Binge-watching the 2016 Cubs-Indians World Series at your own convenience, when the outcome is already known, certainly removes suspense from the sports equation (although I suspect that some Cubs fans, at least, will want to revisit the highlights in winters to come).

It is also important to recognize that baseball has a unique business model in which a large share of income is derived from local cable broadcasts, with the cable stations owned in part or wholly by the team. Although baseball trails the N.F.L. and the N.B.A. in national ratings, its local broadcasts dominate the market in many cities.

Whether games are experienced at the park, on television and radio, or on various mobile devices, the average age of fans would be considerably higher if it were not for a rise in the number of Hispanic fans that parallels the growth of the Hispanic population in the United States. The estimated median age of Hispanic viewers of national baseball telecasts in 2016 was only fifty-one—five years younger than the baseball audience as a whole. A breakdown of the numbers from 2015 shows why. More than 36 percent of Hispanic viewers of national telecasts were under thirty-five, compared with only 21 percent for the audience as a whole.[10] One of the most startling Nielsen statistics is a 30 percent rise in Hispanic viewership of English-language World Series broadcasts in 2015 (when the Kansas City Royals beat the Mets in five games) from 2014 (when the Royals lost to the San Francisco Giants in seven).[11] New York is a much larger market than San Francisco, but Hispanic viewership of regular-season broadcasts, in both English and Spanish, is up throughout the county.

It makes historical sense that more young Americans of Hispanic descent are watching baseball on English-language television. In the 1920s and 1930s, a similar rise in enthusiasm for baseball took place among descendants of Italian and east European Jewish immigrants (as well as among first-generation immigrants themselves, for whom baseball was one pathway into American culture). My grandmother, born in 1899 and the daughter of German immigrants, became a fan not only because of my grandfather's influence but because she was captivated by the career of Lou Gehrig, born in 1903 to German immigrant parents in the Yorkville neighborhood of Manhattan. Even though Gehrig played for the hated Yankees, Gran recalled, she had always cheered when he batted against the Sox in Chicago.

The presence of so many Latinos in baseball—they have made up 25–30 percent of M.L.B. players in recent years—presumably has the same impact on Hispanic Americans as Gehrig did on my grandmother and the desegregation of baseball did on black American fans in the 1950s. At this point in American history, with the Hispanic-American population growing as a result of continuing immigration from Latin America and the increase in the number of American-born descendants of immigrants, the definition of Hispanic is more complex than, say, the definition of an American Jew or an Italian American was in my grandmother's generation. That is true whether one is talking about self-definition or definition of ethnicity by outsiders. That complexity is reflected in the preferences of Hispanic Americans regarding English- and Spanish-language broadcasts (in baseball and other sports). It is no surprise that ESPN Deportes, which broadcasts some 4,500 hours of live Spanish-language sporting events each year, has found that Hispanics gravitate to soccer in Spanish. First-generation immigrants grew up playing and watching soccer in their native lands, and many still root for their favorite teams. American football, by contrast, is often watched by the same people in English—simply because football is identified not with their native countries but with the United States. Baseball is different, because it has a passionate following and cultural roots in both Latin America and the United States.

"When you speak about baseball, it speaks to Latinos on both sides of their being," explains Freddy Rolón, vice president and general manager of ESPN Deportes. "There is a question of identity and how it is mixed between your country of birth and the country you are part of and you live in."[12] Moreover, the Hispanic audience as identified by Nielsen includes many second- and third-generation Americans whose dominant language is English and whose ethnically based emotional ties to baseball may, like my grandmother's, have little to do with real ties to an ancestor's native country. My grandmother's love for Gehrig was based not on any atavistic attachment to Germany but on her pleasure at the success of someone whose background was similar to hers. In similar fashion, the American-born child or grandchild of Hispanic immigrants might idolize Albert Pujols, David Ortiz, or Pedro Martínez while watching the game in English rather than Spanish. In 2015, when Martínez was inducted into the Hall of Fame, on what was Father's Day in the Dominican Republic, he delivered a bilingual acceptance speech that reduced many in the Cooperstown audience to tears.

That baseball speaks to both sides of an American with a Hispanic heritage is an asset rather than a liability for American baseball. "I never feel more American than when I'm watching baseball," says a young friend of mine, a doctor who was born in New York after his parents immigrated (legally) from the Dominican Republic in 1975. "I watch in English because I think in English, but I get an extra kick from seeing Latino players on the field. Part of it is that with all of the disrespectful talk about immigrants today, I know it means a lot to my parents to see us represented in what Americans call their 'national pastime.' Which my parents think is a real joke, since they always considered it the Dominican national pastime. They came with green cards, and it took them eleven years to go through the whole process to become citizens."

If the increase in young Hispanic-American fans is one of baseball's brightest demographic spots, the tepid interest of young African Americans (especially in comparison with their enthusiasm for basketball) is a serious problem. During the 2015 season, only one in five African Americans who tuned into national baseball broadcasts was under thirty-five—compared with more than one in three Hispanics.

The diminution of interest in baseball on the part of young African Americans is, in some measure, attributable to the same social factors that have made many young white (non-Hispanic) Americans call the game "boring." There is no racial segregation when it comes to the shortening of attention spans. Yet in entirely predictable fashion, there is no shortage of white people trying to provide some special, race-related explanation for the erosion of the fan base among people to whom baseball meant a great deal both before and after the color line was breached in 1947.

Some studies and scholars attempt to connect the decline of black participation in baseball with "broken homes" headed by single mothers and the dearth of "fathers playing catch with sons." In the conservative Christian magazine *Canon and Culture,* Evan Lenow, an assistant professor of ethics at Southwestern Baptist Theological Seminary in Fort Worth, even suggests that absent fathers are the main reason why black teenagers choose basketball over baseball. "Basketball requires a hoop and a ball," he writes. "A child can work on the game by himself. Baseball, on the other hand, requires more than one person." Specifically, baseball requires fathers, who are "especially important to boys."[13]

I wish Lenow had been with me last summer in the park near my New York apartment, where I sat down after my morning walk and watched a young mother who lives in my building throwing a ball to her four-year-old son. He had an excellent batting stance for a child so young and made solid contact repeatedly. As it happens, this little boy also has a very-much-present father, but it certainly seems that mothers can play catch with sons too. That is, unless one is determined to blame baseball's twenty-first-century problems, like so much else, on changes in women's and men's roles that disturb the most conservative evangelical Christians.

I would also suggest that there is more enlightenment to be gained on this subject by listening to African Americans than to whites.

Chris Rock, in a 2015 interview with Bryant Gumbel, called himself, a black baseball fan, part of "an endangered species." Rock, who was born in 1965, ticked off a list of reasons why young African Americans are not as involved with baseball as he was when he was growing up. Guess what? Not one of those reasons has anything to do with single mothers. Many of them have to do with the drop in the number of black players in the major leagues since the 1980s. When Rock was coming of age in New York City, the 1986 Mets won the World Series with a team that included several black players who were fan favorites—Darryl Strawberry, Dwight Gooden, Kevin Mitchell, and Mookie Wilson. Wilson was genuinely beloved not only because he was an excellent player who worked ceaselessly to make the most of his talents but because of the obvious joy he displayed on the field. In the interview, aired on HBO, Rock pointed out that the San Francisco Giants had no black players on their starting team when they won the 2014 World Series. He remarked that "the closest thing to a person of color in the stands was their mascot, a biracial seal." Rock also pointed out that many historically black colleges, including Howard University, have sharply cut back on or dispensed with baseball programs altogether. "Yeah," Rock said, "lacrosse is black enough for Howard, but not baseball." Rock also cited many of the same reasons advanced by young whites for their boredom with baseball—including the idea that the game moves too slowly for today's culture.[14]

Of all these explanations, which also appear frequently on sports blogs by black writers, the one that makes the most sense is the decline in the number of African-American players since the late 1980s. I became a conscious baseball fan during the first decade after desegregation, but some of my most vivid youthful images of individual players involve African Americans— Robinson, Ernie Banks, Willie Mays, and Larry Doby. (Doby was the second black player to break the color barrier—with the Cleveland Indians—and played for my White Sox for the better part of the 1956 and 1957 seasons.) The best pitcher I have ever seen personally (by my definition of "best," which means the most relentless competitor) was Bob Gibson, the man whose earned run average was so low that it forced M.L.B. to raise the mound in 1969 to give hitters a chance. Many other African-American players have a permanent place in my memory: Roy Campanella, Henry Aaron, Ozzie Smith, and Reggie Jackson—to name only a few. But these are stars from the past. There is no question that the most important black athletes in recent years—the kind of athletes who enable African-American kids to look up and see themselves—have been in other sports. Baseball today has no LeBron James, no Serena or Venus Williams. As Derrick Clifton, a writer who grew up on Chicago's South Side recalls, there is no substitute—for creating fans or amateurs who enjoy a sport—for seeing athletes of high achievement who enable you to imagine doing what they do.

> And on a personal level, although I'm far from a professional tennis player, I once dreamed about that possibility. As a kid who grew up on Chicago's South Side, I didn't see or notice much about tennis; I was being pushed toward basketball or football. That's until I happened upon Venus playing in the 2000 Wimbledon finals against Lindsay Davenport. . . .

After I saw Venus win, I thought, "Maybe I can play that sport some day." Many of my friends would say something similar after watching the Williams sisters in their youth, as they aged along with them.[15]

It is of more than passing interest, in view of the decline in the number of African-American baseball players since the 1980s, that Derrick Clifton was being pushed toward basketball and football—not baseball—in his black neighborhood on the South Side. Somehow, this does not strike me as the doing of single moms and absent dads. Tony Clark, executive director of the Major League Baseball Players Association, argues that "unfortunately, the MO of our industry has been to promote its teams rather than its stars."[16] Clark is right about that, but rooting for the home team has been a bigger part of the culture of baseball since the beginning than of any other sport. I am not sure, had a hometown superstar in baseball done what James did—leave the Cleveland Cavaliers for four years to play for the Miami Heat—that he would have been welcomed back to Cleveland with the overwhelming enthusiasm James enjoyed in 2014.* But James—like many of basketball's and football's biggest names—is a national figure. There may not have been anyone in baseball like him since Babe Ruth. Also, there is a bias among baseball lifers against stars who are seen as "hot dogs" seeking the limelight for themselves and not their teams. Disdain for the hot dog player runs counter to a celebrity culture that exerts its hold

*Actually, James was born in Akron, Ohio, not in Cleveland—but the two cities are close enough to make him a homegrown hero.

on the young even more strongly than on older Americans. Then too, the bias of baseball's traditionalists against "styling"—such as "showing up" a pitcher by prancing around the bases with obvious, arrogant delight—does not sit well with fans under thirty-five. Americans of many generations enjoy styling. Face it, we are a country that likes seeing football players pound the ball—and one another—in the end zone. And most of us don't much care if a pitcher who has just given up a home run (at least, if the pitcher is on the other team) is "shown up" by a satisfied hitter. This is a *game,* after all, not the negotiation of some dreary business merger. What's not to like about a player who has just hit a home run pouncing emphatically on the plate, joyously doffing his cap to the fans, and throwing a kiss to women in the stands?

One interesting element in the story of the steady decline in the proportion of black major league baseball players since the late 1980s appears in a study published by the Society for American Baseball Research, a group of scholars and writers who have made a great contribution to understanding the game by the numbers. While the percentage of black players rose steadily between 1948 and the late 1980s, it was never as large as reported in many sports articles. The figure that used to be cited for African-American players in the 1980s was around 30 percent; in fact, it was closer to 19 percent. The reason: dark-skinned Hispanic players were counted as "black"—by baseball as well as outside analysts.[17] The longtime practice of judging a player's ethnicity purely by skin color is one nasty way in which baseball was indeed just like American life. There is no question, though, that the percentage of African-American players has dropped sharply since the early 1990s. In 1986, African Americans made up 18.3 percent of players on opening-day rosters; in 2017, the figure was 7.7 percent.[18]

M.L.B. cannot escape its share of responsibility for the drop in African-American participation since the 1980s, because it is cheaper to train and sign young players in Latin American countries than in the United States. Rock did make one feckless, uninformed comment in his interview when he dismissed the expense of baseball training for teenagers as a factor in the decline of black participation. He observed that poor Dominicans play baseball and that the "only equipment they have are twigs for bats, diapers for gloves and Haitians for bases."[19] Perhaps Rock was thinking of toddlers when he was talking about "diapers for gloves," because the most talented Dominican teenagers have access to academies financed by all American major league clubs.

Although the decline in the proportion of African-American players is a perennial bad news story in baseball, there are some signs that the trend may be changing. According to figures provided by Pat Courtney, assistant to Commissioner of Baseball Rob Manfred, nine of thirty-six first-round draft picks in 2015 were African American—the largest proportion since 1992. M.L.B. attributes a significant part of this increase to the impact of its urban youth academies. Manfred expects the results of the youth academy training to be felt at the major league level within the next few years. If the programs continue to produce more first-round draft picks, there are likely to be more African Americans on opening-day rosters by, say, 2020. "To call this a high priority would be an understatement," Manfred says. "It's important for teams, it's important for attracting new fans."[20] The 7.7 percent of African-American players on opening-day rosters in 2017 was up a full percentage point from 2016—a number worth mentioning if only because it suggests much-needed movement in the right direction.

Women are another demographic sore spot for baseball, which has a smaller proportion of female fans than any other major sport. This is a genuinely baffling phenomenon, since girls and young women are much more involved with all sports than at any time in the past.

Many more women watch nationally televised football during the regular season than baseball (6.2 million compared with 141,000 in 2015). The total audience for football is much larger than for baseball, but even on a percentage basis, baseball has the smallest share of female fans of any major sport. According to the National Football League, women make up approximately 45 percent of the sport's huge fan base. Year after year, the Super Bowl is the single most watched television program by women as well as men.[21]

I admit that I don't get it. Why on earth should NASCAR have a higher proportion of female fans than baseball? (Don't tell me it's because girls just love hot cars.) The failure of baseball to attract more female fans, at a time when girls are more interested than previous generations in a wide variety of sports, is a mystery that must be solved if baseball is to maintain its status in the future—not necessarily as *the* national pastime but as one of the nation's most important and emotionally resonant pastimes.

I once introduced a brilliant Russian-born scientist to base-ball, and it took him a full year before he understood enough to enjoy the play on the field with anything like the gusto of someone whose summers were once defined by rhythms trans-lated into numbers in daily box scores. Later he became a serious fan—more Catholic than the pope in his devotion to what still, in the early 1970s, seemed like the most meaningful ritual of his adopted country. He thanked me but admitted that he would never have persevered in his baseball education had I not been his first American girlfriend. "I thought you had to understand this game to please American women," he confessed. "It's the thinking person's game, and I just assumed it would appeal to women who want cleverness instead of violence out of a sport."

I found this an interesting observation from someone looking at baseball from the outside, and he was surprised to find that very few of the women he met had any interest in baseball. That girls are unlikely to play baseball at the professional level is ir-relevant: women are certainly not going to play N.F.L. football or N.H.L. hockey in their current forms. Basketball and soccer, of course, are quite different, because women can and do play both sports at a high professional level (even though they do not make as much money as men). But people become sports fans not because they really believe (at least after, say, age twelve) that they are going to play professionally but because they be-came interested in and often played the game as a child. Young girls play both softball and hardball—at least before pushy parents and coaches start taking over in middle school and telling the children to get serious about the future. The At Bat program for children of all ages throughout the country, sponsored by M.L.B. and USA Baseball (the governing body of amateur sports) is designed to teach children how to have fun playing games that involve catching, throwing, and hitting—from wiffle ball to hardball. The emphasis is on playing rather than winning (in contrast to tightly structured programs like Little League).

There is one enormously powerful and logical reason why baseball could and should appeal to a larger female base: it is a much safer game than either football or hockey for children who participate in sports. The publicity about concussions in football, not only in the N.F.L. but at the high school level, is already having an impact on the willingness of parents (fathers as well as mothers) to allow their sons to play high school football. Donald Trump mocks concern about concussions as an example of the sissification of America and has called the N.F.L. "weak" for instituting new rules to protect players who display concussion symptoms.[22] However, ordinary middle-class parents—including some famous former N.F.L. players suffering the aftereffects of traumatic brain injury—don't feel that way. Baseball occasionally produces concussions, but, unlike football, is not designed to be a bruising contact sport. When concussions do happen in baseball, they happen by accident—because someone has made a mistake—rather than as the inevitable result of the way the game is played. The quotient of built-in physical combat in football and hockey (though not in basketball) is much higher than that of baseball at both the middle school and high school level.

Mothers (even those with jobs, *pace Canon and Culture*) still do more of the driving than fathers to practice sessions for their children, and I would be nauseated after dropping off my son at a practice where he could be at risk for a serious head injury. Knowing what we know today about the effect of concussions on young teenagers, I am proud that my parents refused to let my younger brother, who was unusually small for his age, play football when he entered high school. They had the courage of their convictions before there was medical proof, and it wasn't easy to say no in central Michigan's football-saturated environment. It is easier to say no today because there is medical proof, and baseball should make that a selling point for mothers and fathers.

The estrangement of many women from baseball (like the attitudes of many young African Americans toward the game) cannot be divorced from history. The pieces of history affecting women are not as well known as the racial and racist history of the game, and they are surely unknown to most Americans under forty. The baseball establishment's long history of inhospitality to female members of the media, and much of the male media's denigration of female fans and women's knowledge of the game, should not be overlooked. Roger Angell, chronicling baseball for the *New Yorker*, was one of the few writers to explore this subject with depth and sensitivity in the 1970s. At that time, female sportswriters, inspired by the twentieth-century wave of American feminism, were fighting for the right to interview players in locker rooms. (The issue eventually had to be resolved in court.) They encountered much stronger resistance from baseball players than from professional hockey or basketball players. Baseball's long season, with games played nearly every day (half of them on the road) for six months, places players in an all-male world for much longer periods than any other sport. There was a strong tradition of "what happens on the road stays on the road," and female reporters were seen by many players and managers as potential Trojan horses who either would tattle on cheating husbands to their wives at home or would distract players from their job by seducing them. Players who wanted their wives to travel with them, even to postseason games, were often mocked. In 1979, Angell wrote:

> It seems to me that the people who run sports and who claim to be most concerned about the "sexual privacy" of their athletes in the clubhouse—surely one of the most sexless and joyless surroundings in which men and women can meet—are men who want to keep both sports and sex in some safe, special place where they first locked them up when they were adolescents. The new presence of capable, complicated women in the inner places of sports means that relations between the sexes cannot be relegated just to marriage, or just to hotel rooms either.[23]

I saw what the first generation of female baseball writers endured during the 1970s and 1980s, and I am glad that many of the young women I know find these stories difficult to believe. Claire Smith, now a respected news editor for ESPN, was awarded the highest honor of the Baseball Writers Association of America—the J. G. Taylor Spink Award—and then honored in the summer of 2017 at the Baseball Hall of Fame for her "meritorious contributions to sportswriting." The recognition came thirty-two years after Smith, then a baseball writer for the *Hartford Courant,* had been barred from the San Diego Padres' clubhouse after the first game of the 1984 National League Championship Series with the Cubs. Fearful that she would miss her deadline, Smith was crying and sent a message to the Padres' Steve Garvey, who had opposed banning female reporters from the locker room. Garvey came outside to talk to her. Kristie Ackert of the *New York Daily News,* one of five female members of the Baseball Writers' Association whom Smith asked to stand with her when she received the Spink Award, recounts that Garvey told Smith not to cry—"that she was just doing her job and despite what happened, she had the right to [do her work] and had plenty of support."[24] Smith persevered, and she was a pioneer not only as a woman but as an African-American baseball writer on many newspapers. "In New York, she paved the way for me," writes Ackert, who now covers the Mets for the *News.* "And she paid an enormous emotional price."[25]

The disdain with which many male baseball writers used to regard women as fans and as reporters was expressed by the late Jerome Holtzman, a writer for the *Chicago Sun-Times* who was considered the unofficial "dean of sportswriters" by his contemporary colleagues. "The press box used to be a male preserve— that was its charm," Holtzman said. "I'd rather not have a woman as a seatmate at a World Series game. It wouldn't be as much fun. I never met a woman who knew as much baseball as a man."[26] It hurt me to read that; it made me wonder whether some of the men who went to games with me felt the same way. It hurt so much that I was able to find the quotation immediately in a thick book I had not looked at for decades.

I don't know how many men today—and men still control most of the history and management of major league baseball—share Holtzman's views, and there has certainly been a decline in sex discrimination in every aspect of sports since the 1980s. I suspect, however, that the lingering odor of such sentiments does have an effect even on young women who have never been exposed personally to the blatant sexism faced by Claire Smith's generation of baseball-loving females. It is possible to feel like an outsider (or perhaps someone who has only one foot in the door) even though an institution's social policies and the attitudes of the participants have changed.

In fact, some antifemale attitudes—on the part of both fans and those who run the game's finances and broadcasting—have persisted in ways that might make a woman feel that this is 1958, not 2018. On the occasion of Smith's Spink Award, Doug Glanville, a former outfielder for the Cubs, Phillies, and Texas Rangers and a former color analyst on baseball for ESPN, wrote a remarkably frank column in the *New York Times* about the sexism directed at his colleague Jessica Mendoza in the broadcast booth. He observed that Mendoza, an Olympic gold medalist in softball, never has the advantage of beginning any sentence in the broadcast booth with, "When I played for the Chicago Cubs." Mendoza, who is highly respected by her broadcasting colleagues, constantly attracts comments on social media implying that she knows nothing about the game because she never played in the major leagues. Among the comments reported by

Glanville: "She doesn't belong in the booth with men discussing a game she knows nothing about. It's like watching a game with a girlfriend." Glanville makes the telling observation that while Mendoza is often dismissed by envious social media couch potatoes because she never played major league ball, countless male sportscasters—among them the legendary Vin Scully—also never played the game at any demanding amateur, much less professional, level. In two particularly eloquent paragraphs, Glanville summed up the attitude that baseball needs to project in order to attract more female fans:

> Sports, on and off the field, should set an example for fairness, decency and humanity for all of our children, not just the legacy of boys already in the boys club. Sports are loved by so many of us, and we need to appreciate that everyone has a story to tell about the games we love. Yes, women too.
>
> I don't know whether Jessica Mendoza will become the next Vin Scully. Even Vin Scully didn't know he would be the next Vin Scully. But I would like to give trailblazers a chance to make it happen, because they move mountains—and people, some of whom have had to overcome significant obstacles. In Cooperstown, after decades of male faces on the wall of Spink Award recipients, Claire Smith's face will now shift history.[27]

The men who run baseball today do recognize the economic importance of female fans—particularly when it comes to ball-park attendance. "Every study tells us that women control discretionary spending on recreation for families," says Manfred. "That means baseball games. We want women to come to games with their families for that obvious reason, apart from the fact that we want baseball to have the widest and most diverse audience possible. And when moms come to the ballpark, a lot more kids come too. Again, it's obvious." The enthusiasm with which both male and female fans greeted the star performance of fourteen-year-old Mo'ne Davis—one of two girls to play in the 2014 Little League World Series—gives a hint of the possibilities that M.L.B. could develop. Even though it is unlikely that a woman will ever play major league baseball, human beings of both sexes can understand and love a game because it embodies multiple possibilities of excellence. A woman's place is in a major league ballpark, just as a man's place is in a tennis stadium watching Serena Williams.

The definition of a true fan is not someone who finds it imperative to go out to the ballgame once—or even more times—a week. No one ever had the chance to be that kind of fan unless he or she was retired or possessed considerable wealth; at the height of my enthusiasm for the Mets in the 1980s, when I shared a season ticket, I never went to more than seven games in a season. I watched many more games on television or listened to them on radio in the middle of the night when the team was on the West Coast. For the most part—unless there was a crucial series—I watched or listened to no more than two games a week. It is possible to be too much of a fan—to be addicted to sports in passive, couch-potato fashion. In 2015–16, according to Nielsen, Americans spent a "shocking" number of hours—more than 31 billion—viewing athletic events on television. Shocking is the right word—and that figure does not include any of the time people spend viewing games, or more likely moments of games, on mobile devices. But there is no evidence that viewing or listening to games away from the ballpark has ever discouraged people from attending live games. Go to a ballpark anywhere in the country (unless you happen to live on Chicago's North Side, on a block that is only a ten-minute walk from Wrigley Field), and you are committing yourself to a long commute in addition to the three-hour game. Getting out to Citi Field, the home of the Mets, takes about an hour by subway from where I live in Manhattan (that is, if there are no signal breakdowns on the Lexington Avenue line, which I must take to Grand Central Terminal to change for the Flushing line to the Mets' ballpark in Flushing, Queens). Need I add that the ride seems even longer after a loss? (This expedition proved to be a bit too challenging for some of the men who attended the 2017 convention of the Society for American Baseball Research in New York. The *New York Times* reported some of the grumbling by the sabermetricians about having to take the subway, and the article was accompanied by a hilarious picture of a panel whose attendees seemed to consist almost entirely of middle-aged white men with paunches.)[28]

The availability of television to watch games in the comfort of my own home has never discouraged me from attending live games, which provide a very different visual and emotional experience. Instead, I have always been grateful that live games are only one choice enabling me to follow the sport I love, at times when going out to the ballpark is literally impossible.

Even when I was a child, attending games with my grandparents fed my appetite for taking in games on radio and television at home, and vice versa. Baseball fans, it must be acknowledged, include more than a few snobs who talk as if the only "real" way to watch a game were at the park and who pretend that they never, ever turn from the news to a sports channel, flop on the couch, and tune out a chaotic, lawless world for a time in order to watch a world with well-defined rules. There is a pretentiousness about this resembling the rigorous nostalgia of Jacques Barzun when he rejected baseball in the 1990s because the business, if not the actual game, did not comport with his memories of America in the 1950s. Baseball is hospitable to fans in a wide variety of formats and platforms (how easily digital language seeps into a sentence about a nondigital subject), but the game cannot prosper in the future as it prospers today if it does not attract the fans who are missing not only from ballparks but from the camaraderie of watching with friends and family in their own homes. A truly American game cannot be the province mainly of old white men—whether on the field or in the stands. I think of what Buck O'Neil, a star first baseman and manager in the American Negro League and the first black coach in major league baseball, said at Satchel Paige's funeral in 1982. In his eulogy, O'Neil addressed one pointed sentence to white Americans: "Don't feel sorry for us," he said, speaking about all of the great black players who were barred from major league baseball before 1947. "I feel sorry for your fathers and mothers, because they didn't get to see us play."[29] What O'Neil had to say about the baseball fan base in an era of involuntary exclusion can be turned around and applied just as aptly to the voluntary exclusion that circumscribes the audience in so many ways today—by race, ethnicity, age and gender. Numbers can lie, but in this instance they tell the truth.

4 the long game and impatient minds

This is a game to be savored, not gulped.

—BILL VEECK

I f there is one area of agreement among all who consider baseball boring or anachronistic, it is that the games are too long and the pace within games is too slow. Run a Google search with the words "baseball games too long and too slow," and more than twenty-two million results pop up. Young men who play fantasy baseball, managing mythical teams drafted on-line with mythical lineups, talk about how wonderful it is to have a baseball experience without wasting three hours at a time on a real game. Old duffers recall that when they were young, games never lasted more than two hours. (This isn't true, unless you are among the few living Americans born in the first decade of the twentieth century, but it's what many people over, roughly, age sixty tend to think.) As for the young, they just say the games are too slow. Bill Veeck (1914–86), the maverick American League owner, who at times ran the St. Louis Browns, the Cleveland Indians, and the Chicago White Sox, followed the quote that introduces this chapter with another pertinent observation. "There's time to discuss everything between pitches and between innings," he told Thomas Boswell of the *Washington Post*. "Baseball is a game that encourages our natural gregariousness."[1] One can only imagine what Veeck would have thought of proposals to quicken the pace of games by turning a foul ball into strike three. (I will digress here and say that Veeck was a Chicago character and institution. He even made it to my grandfather's bar, and his autographed picture occupied a place of honor near the cash register.) Veeck's father was a sportswriter and onetime president of the Cubs, and after the younger Veeck's stints as the owner of the Browns and Indians, he turned up in Chicago again in 1959 as the head of a syndicate that bought a majority interest in the White Sox. In Cleveland, Veeck had brought up Larry Doby, the first black player in the American League, shortly after Jackie Robinson made his debut in Brooklyn. The owner received twenty thousand pieces of hate mail and answered them all by hand.[2] Veeck's return to Chicago as an owner in 1959 gave me my favorite childhood baseball year, as the Sox won the American League pennant. We were beaten by the Los Angeles Dodgers four games to two, but the highlight of the series for me was the fifth game, when my Sox beat Sandy Koufax 1–0. In fairness, it must be noted that the Koufax of 1959, who had an ERA of 4.05, was not the Koufax whose Hall of Fame stature is based on his dominating performances that began in the 1961 season. Still, beating even the pre-Koufax Koufax meant something if you were a Sox fan.

Veeck was, as his comments to Boswell suggest, a famous conversationalist himself, combining humor and the erudition of a voracious reader. He was also one of the few owners who actually liked talking to reporters, so much of his conversation has made it into print. My favorite Veeck story is told by the longtime *New York Daily News* writer Mike Lupica in a column about the 1983 World Series, which brought together three great alumni from Cincinnati's "big Red Machine" of the 1970s. Pete Rose, Tony Pérez, and Joe Morgan were all playing for the Philadelphia Phillies in 1983. Lupica remarked that he was glad the former Reds stars had one more chance to play together, even though they didn't win the series against the Baltimore Orioles. "I've got a poem that fits," Veeck informed Lupica. He wrote out lines from Robert Browning's "Home-Thoughts, from Abroad," including the following: *That's the wise thrush; he sings his song twice over/Lest you should think he could not recapture/The first fine careless rapture.* Lupica checked out the text and found that Veeck had gotten two words wrong. When Lupica called to tell him, Veeck was pleased that he had remembered so much of a poem he had probably read more than four decades earlier. "Memory's a wonderful thing, don't you think," Veeck said.[3]

Veeck's observations form more than a digression, because they cut to the heart of the controversy over the pace of games. Conversation, for every serious fan, is a part of the game itself, and pauses are assets rather than liabilities. Yet conversation itself has been one of the many cultural casualties of the computer era. The Internet, which provides unprecedented opportunities for communication, is also responsible for the most extensive array of conversation avoidance devices in human history. As essayist Stephen Miller observes in a lively history of conversation, these conversation stoppers include not only obvious isolators like video games and anything with headphones but smartphones, e-mail, and text messaging.[4] Paradoxically, while these messaging devices facilitate instrumental communication, they discourage real conversation—what takes place between innings or pitches. Without conversation—whether one is watching a game on a screen or at the ballpark—a game of any length seems long. Talk—not phony movie dialogue about what Shoeless Joe Jackson's ghost might be thinking—is what fills the "silences" between pitches for those watching the game among friends.

The difficulty in analyzing what might seem, on the surface, to be a straightforward subject—with statisticians the undisputed "experts"—is that much of what is written about the length of games confuses the time between the first and last pitch with what can be a slow, quiet pace within a given game. To many of the men who run baseball, the time between pitches that Veeck would fill with conversation is time wasted—time that discourages millennials from coming to the park or from watching an entire game on any screen, anywhere. Commissioner Rob Manfred, in a simmering disagreement with the Major League Baseball Players Association over possible rule changes to shorten the game, says flatly, "I reject the notion that we can 'educate fans' to embrace the game as it's currently played."[5] This is a broad statement, and if Manfred is right, tweaking rules and customs is not likely to ameliorate the situation. The commissioner made his comment during 2017 spring training, after Tony Clark, executive director of the players' union, expressed opposition to major rule changes, such as the imposition of a pitch clock, designed to speed up the pace of the game. Instead of seeing pauses between pitches as a dead zone, Clark told reporters that baseball should use that time to educate fans about the nuances of the game. He said that while he understood "on the surface" why someone might suggest that cutting an extra five, ten, or thirty minutes from the game was a good idea, baseball would do better to find ways of elucidating exactly what is going on during the pauses and silences that punctuate continuous play. He argued that "there's an opportunity to engage, teach, and flip the conversation in a way that allows folks to appreciate what you're seeing."[6]

This dispute is really about the understanding, education, and attention span of younger fans and not about the actual length or pace of games. The average length of an M.L.B. game in 2016 was three hours, four minutes—up from three hours in 2015, but down from the average time in 2014 of three hours and seven minutes. In 1997, the average game took two hours and fifty-two minutes. These averages are the result of adding in the additional time of extra-inning games. The average *nine-inning* game in 2016 lasted only three hours and fifty-one *seconds*.[7] (The original statistics are all derived from Baseball-Reference.com, a gold mine of information about every aspect of the game.)

Does anyone seriously think that a baseball fan is going to reject the game because it takes ten or fifteen minutes more to end today than it did in 1994? If you think a three-hour, four-minute game is boring, two hours and fifty-two minutes will hardly seem more exciting. The 2017 season began with two changes designed to speed up the in-game pace, agreed on by M.L.B. and the players' union. First, the four-pitch intentional walk is no more. Instead, the manager signals the umpire and the batter takes first base. To be honest, I am not enough of a traditionalist to pull out my hair over this change, despite having enjoyed the few occasions on which I have seen a runner score from third base because of a wild pitch thrown during what was supposed to be a routine intentional walk. But the idea that this change will have any significant impact on the length of games —or make kids feel the pace of the game is faster and therefore more exciting—is ridiculous. Here is one of the many places where the sometimes-annoying proliferation of baseball statistics doesn't deceive. In 2016, pitchers issued 932 intentional walks. That adds up to 3,728 pitches over 2,428 regular-season games— or 1.54 extra pitches per game.[8] I'd wager the few dollars I would ever be willing to invest in sports betting that the game minus the intentional walk will last—guess what?—around three hours.

Some changes responding to fan gripes about not-so-instant replays could—I emphasize *could*—have a slightly—very slightly —greater effect. Managers now have a thirty-second limit to initiate a replay challenge, and there is a theoretical two-minute limit on the time replay officials have to study the tape and announce whether the initial call has been upheld or overturned. But there will be exceptions in special circumstances, so the ten-minute replay—which can affect some pitchers' control and composure as they stand around—may not be a thing of the past. And my guess is that a typical game will still last, yes, about three hours. So why the never-ending kerfuffle about the length and pacing of games? The veteran sportswriter George Vecsey tartly observes, alluding to the steroid era, "The owners didn't notice when their sluggers' craniums and jawbones kept growing. Now the owners notice when an occasional game goes too long?"[9] I suspect that most of the talk about the games being too long and the pacing too slow is a substitute for the specter that hangs over the future of today's prosperous game—the loss of young people who do not understand what is really going on in a quiet, seemingly endless ten-pitch battle between the man on the mound and the hitter at the plate. It is easier to talk about tweaks, such as limiting the number of times a hitter can step out of the batter's box, as a way to make millennial fans feel that things are moving along at a pace they might prefer than it is to face up to the cultural forces that make it difficult for the young to pay attention when the action in the game is subtle rather than obvious. In fact, the 2018 season is likely to begin with some type of pitch clock limiting the amount of time a pitcher can take before he releases the ball, because the current contract between the players' union and M.L.B. gives the commissioner the right to impose a number of changes in pacing without the assent of the union. The concerns of those who see, in these seemingly small changes, a slippery slope that could lead to the end of what makes baseball special were expressed during the 2017 All-Star break by the reliever Pat Neshek. Neshek predicted that following the introduction of the pitch clock, "there will be something after that. And something after that. And 50 years from now, we'll ask, 'How did we get to this point?' It'll be the little things like this."[10]

We shall see whether the imposition of time limits on a timeless game will actually shorten playing time and whether young fans will even notice if a game is, say, fifteen minutes shorter than three hours.

An interesting example of the confusion between length and boredom appears on Nate Silver's fivethirtyeight.com Web site, one of the premier forums for statistical analysis of everything from sports to politics. The article, written during the cliffhanging 2016 World Series, was titled, "Baseball's Biggest Games Are Taking Forever," and it analyzed the reasons why postseason games are generally longer than regular-season games.[11] As is the wont of sabermetricians, the author had the time of the October games down to the minute—an average of three hours and twenty-four minutes, compared with three hours, two minutes for the regular season.* I am not interested in having "big games" last as long as possible—particularly when, as is the case with so many of these contests, the first ball is not thrown until between 8:15 and 8:30 p.m. Eastern Daylight Time. Starting these games earlier in the evening or, on weekends, in the daytime would probably be the most effective way to introduce a new generation of children, at a time when they can still keep their eyes open, to baseball at its highest level. But we know that isn't going to happen, because television sponsors are interested in pitching their products at a time when the coveted 18-to-34 demographic is most likely to be watching.

Writing after two games of the 2016 Series, fivethirtyeight's Rob Arthur attributed the length of the game to the use of more relievers and to the tendency of relievers to take more time between pitches than starters. He noted that there had been 4.06 relief appearances per game at that point in the postseason, compared with a regular-season average of 3.14 per game. "Each

---

*You may recall that Baseball-Reference.com declared the average to be three hours, four minutes for regular-season games. Never mind.

pitching change can take up to two minutes and 30 seconds," he explains, "so pitcher usage accounts for another two- to three-minute chunk of the sluggish pace." Take note of the difference, which is just two to three minutes. Relief pitchers also take more time between pitches—approximately 1.7 seconds more per throw—than starters, so "we've accounted for another 25 or so extra seconds per game."[12] Does this really matter? When all of the too-long games were over, the Cubs-Indians Series attracted the largest number of fans in sixteen years. People don't tune out a great game because a relief pitcher is taking 1.7 seconds more between pitches than a starter. They tune out, in both the literal and metaphoric senses, when a game seems hopelessly one-sided.

I never tuned out one minute of the best, most thrilling game I have ever seen, which lasted four hours and forty-two minutes and took sixteen innings to determine the winner of the 1986 National League pennant. It was played in Houston on Wednesday, October 15, 1986, between the Houston Astros and the Mets—the sixth and what turned out to be decisive game in the League Championship Series. The unusual weekday afternoon start was mandated by M.L.B. because the game had to be finished before 8 p.m. in the East to make way for the American League contest scheduled in Boston, between the Red Sox and the California Angels. New York fans unlucky enough to be stuck in their offices followed the first half of the marathon through surreptitious phone calls to friends who happened to be at home. When it grew late enough in the day to leave work, many people looked for television sets—whether in the windows of stores or in bars—instead of heading straight home. (This was, of course, before smartphones, which would have rendered all of the torturous efforts to keep in touch with the action unnecessary.) I was working (to use the term loosely) at home that day, but my partner Luke (whose name has been changed in the interest of privacy) was in his office until around five o'clock. His bosses had been inconsiderate enough to schedule a meeting with out-of-town clients before anyone knew that there would be an important ballgame that day. Nevertheless, we were on the phone every twenty minutes, as I reported the mainly bad news about the Mets during the first eight innings. I told him not to worry about missing this game, because the Mets had been behind 3–0 since the first inning. We had already made plans to watch the seventh, deciding game together the next day, and no one was more surprised than Luke when he walked through my door at some point between 5:30 and 6 o'clock and found me watching the tenth inning of a tie game. Between the time he had left his office and taken the subway to the stop near my apartment, the Mets had scored three runs in the ninth inning. We would watch the last six innings together.

It was awful, it was wonderful, I will never forget that time out of time as long as I live.

Although the Mets were leading the series three games to two, the pressure was on them, because the Astros' starting pitcher the next day would be Mike Scott, a right-handed master of the split-fingered fastball. Suspicions that he scuffed the ball with sandpaper had been voiced by many players and managers. He had been the master of the Mets, and, as every fan knew, the looming presence of Scott made game 6 seem like game 7 to the New York team. Wally Backman, the Mets second baseman, inspected some of Scott's foul balls (which the team had actually been collecting) and said, "I don't think grass can do that to a baseball. Here's one where he got both sides. Only sandpaper can do that. I guess you could say he had his good 'scuff' tonight."[13] According to one writer, Scott, regardless of what he "was or wasn't doing to the baseball . . . had clearly reduced the Mets' psyche to marginal paranoia."[14]

The box score for the game is a beautiful diagram, showing the Astros' three runs in the first inning and the Mets' three runs in the ninth. Otherwise, eight boxes of zeros for the Mets, eight boxes of zeros for the Astros. Then the lines of zeros for both teams in the tenth, eleventh, twelfth, and thirteenth innings. In the fourteenth, the Mets scored one run but left two men on base. The Astros tied the game in their half of the inning when the normally light-hitting outfielder Billy Hatcher lined a home run—fair, just barely, after hitting the foul pole—off the Mets' ace reliever Jesse Orosco.* The fifteenth was another scoreless inning, and then came the sixteenth—in which the Mets scored three runs in their half. In my living room and in the Houston Astrodome, it should have felt as if the game was over—but somehow it didn't. Too many improbable reversals had already occurred.

---

*If a ball touches the foul pole before it lands in the stands, it is considered a "fair" home run. At least once a year, some announcer insists that the "foul" pole should really be called the "fair" pole. Those announcers have a point.

Orosco, who was the Mets' closer and usually pitched only one inning, was clearly exhausted as he took the mound for the sixteenth. Luke and I, our beers nearly untouched because we agreed, with unapologetic irrationality, that it was good luck to lick foam but bad luck to actually drink between pitches, could hardly bear to look at the television screen as Orosco gave up two runs in the Astros' half of the inning. Then, with the tying run at second base for Houston, Orosco threw a slider to the Astros' switch-hitting outfielder Kevin Bass. Bass struck out. Final score: Mets 7, Houston 6. Luke and I jumped up off the couch, yelped like children, and threw our arms around each other, as similar joyful noises reached us through the open windows from every other apartment building on my block. Everyone who had been at the office when the game began had obviously made it to a refuge with a television long before the end. Then Luke poured our flat, warm beer into the sink, opened the refrigerator, and pulled out a split of champagne, which he had concealed under his suit jacket when he arrived at the beginning of the tenth inning. Expecting to find that the Mets had lost after my last gloomy phone call in the seventh inning before he left the office, Luke bought the champagne to express his hope that we would be able to celebrate tomorrow. We celebrated right then. The sixth game would not have been more fun had it been shorter; part of the pleasure lay in the tension of a contest tied, then re-tied, then almost tied again at the last minute (literally). I am not saying that I would want every game, or even many games, to last this long in either the regular season or the postseason. But this particular game, which reminded me then and still reminds me of Cole Porter's 1934 song "You're the Top," needed every second of every minute of every inning to produce the thrill of it all. ✓

I realize—oh, how often I have heard it—that this all sounds childish to anyone who finds baseball boring. "Childish" is the wrong word, I tell them. What the occasional "you're the top" game does is provide a fan with a child*like* feeling of wonder, of going along for a ride you can't control and loving it. Philip Roth, in his 1991 memoir *Patrimony,* describes the same game, which he experienced from London via transatlantic phone conversations with his father in New Jersey. Herman Roth had been seriously ill that spring, and his son had attempted to divert him by reviving his interest in baseball.

When Philip calls around 11:30 p.m. London time, expecting the game to be over, he asks his father, "Well, what happened?" Herman replies, "It's still on. You wouldn't believe it. Thirteenth inning." Then he adds, "It's beautiful." Philip, of course, cannot go to sleep and gets out of bed around midnight to place another call to New Jersey. The game is still not over, and Herman gives his son a play-by-play account of the action at what used to be expensive transatlantic telephone rates.

So Philip finally goes back to bed and tells his father he will call the next day to learn how it all came out. But Herman can't wait; he phones Philip at 7 a.m. his time, noon London time, to tell him the Mets won in sixteen innings. He has just read an account of the game in the morning paper, which reports that after Orosco (whom the elder Roth calls "Morosco") gave up two runs in the sixteenth, Keith Hernandez went out to the mound and told the pitcher to use his best pitch, the slider. "If you throw another fastball, I'll kill you," Hernandez reportedly said. "I wonder if he would have," Philip says and then recalls Herman's reply. "'*I* would have,' my father said, laughing, and sounding as though whatever had floored him in the spring was a fluke and he was going to live a thousand years."[15]

That's it. Baseball is a team game that never allows a fan to take his or her eyes off the individual, and what one sees in the weary arm of an Orosco (who was then only twenty-nine) is how difficult the game is to play, how fallible and mortal its participants are. In a strange way, the aging-related fallibility of one's favorite players offers a glimpse of the mental toughness that, if only for a moment, defines a mensch at any age. I understand why Herman Roth sounded at that moment to his son like a man who was going to live a thousand years. I understand because I felt the same way myself during the long afternoon's journey into night that was the sixth game of the 1986 National League Championship series. Watching it all with someone I loved—someone who appreciated the excellence of what he was seeing as I appreciated it—deepened the joy. To experience something wondrous, and know at the time that it is something wondrous, is rare. It is part of the long game.

Needless to say, many bloggers, sportswriters, and casual fans who find the game too slow, as well as baseball officials, have all sorts of suggestions that would make it impossible for a game like the 1986 battle between the Mets and Astros ever to be played again. In a special feature "objectively" titled "Baseball's Slow.

Too Slow. Here's How to Fix It," the *New York Times* invited sportswriters and readers to pass along their solutions in search of a problem. One brilliant suggestion from Robert Azar of Brooklyn was that after eleven innings, the home team should be able to pull its best hitter out of the dugout—even if he had already played and been taken out of the game. The visiting team would then be able to pick its pitcher to face the home team's slugger in a ten-pitch home run derby. If the slugger hits a home run, the home team wins. If he doesn't, the visiting team wins. What a brilliant idea! Turn games that matter into one-on-one contests that have nothing to do with the complex game baseball actually is. This change would overturn the foundation of baseball—the fact that you can never, at any point, just "run out the clock." Each team must always get the other team out three times, whether in the first or the sixteenth inning. That is what makes baseball different from other sports. It is why most of the Houston fans stayed in their seats in the Astrodome when their team was down by three runs in the bottom of the sixteenth inning. It is why, when the Astros scored twice, Luke and I were yelling at the television screen before Orosco threw his last, cruel slider to Bass. Many readers who wrote to the *Times* seemed fixated not so much on speeding up the game as on making it more like football. "Easy fix," wrote Larry Sternbach of Marlboro, New Jersey, who suggested that baseball have separate offensive and defensive lineups as the N.F.L. does. Then, he argued, major league baseball would "get more hitting, more base running, more scoring, more excitement!" From Boulder, Colorado, Tom Jones proposed that players rotate one position each inning, as in volleyball. This change, Jones said, would make players "better rounded" and "the disproportionate importance of pitchers would disappear."[16] It was tough to tell how many of these suggestions were serious and how many tongue-in-cheek, but they had one element in common: each would turn baseball into an entirely different game. I particularly like the idea of reducing the "disproportionate importance of pitchers." The baseball-volleyball team would be something like a skyscraper with a rotating team of architectural engineers assigned to the plans for each floor. So what if the specifications for the foundation are started by one person and finished by another? It will all work out. It will be exciting to see what happens as the building goes up.

Another frequently ridiculed idea is, in fact, taken seriously by many fans, and it comes straight from the long-ago days when kids actually did play outdoor pickup games at the end of their block. If the game was lasting too long, and it was getting close to the time when our mothers were going to call us home for dinner, we would simply start every inning with a runner at second base. This, again, has been proposed mainly as a solution to the nonproblem of extra-inning games. But the proposal is more than blog-chat; baseball actually began to try it out in 2017 at the rookie level of the minor leagues. The experiment was approved by Joe Torre, the respected former manager who is now M.L.B.'s chief baseball officer. "It's not fun to watch when you go through your whole pitching staff and wind up bringing in a utility infielder to pitch," Torre said. "As much as it's nice to talk about being at an 18-inning game, it takes time."[17]

Shame on you, Joe Torre. And shame on the reporters who did not ask you how many times, during your managerial career, were you forced to bring in a utility infielder to pitch? In 2016, only 185 of 2,428 regular season games went into extra innings. Of those 185 games, two-thirds ended in ten or eleven innings. Only one—count 'em, one—extra-inning game ended with a position player on the mound.[18] So we are talking about a radical change that, at the major league level, would have affected only sixty games in 2016—and only one in the doomsday scenario put forth by Torre. This experiment in the minor leagues, like the extra-inning home run derbies suggested by a fan to the *Times,* is a rule change that would affect the fundamental ethos of baseball, which dictates that every base be earned as well as that every team gets three outs an inning. I suspect—a suspicion based not on sabermetrics but on my unshakable conviction that bad ideas are almost never abandoned once given a chance—that we will have more experimenting with starting runners on second base in extra innings.* What starts at the lower minor league level doesn't necessarily stay on that level. Baseball is scared about its declining proportion of young fans, but talking about "solu-

---

*The one exception I can recall in my lifetime to the rule that bad ideas are extremely durable was Coca-Cola's swift reconsideration of its 1985 decision to abandon its century-old formula and replace it with something called "New Coke." The company announced the abandonment of its original formula on April 23, 1985. On June 11, 1985—after hearing from enraged customers who hated the new formula—the company put its old Coke back on the supermarket shelves as "Coca-Cola Classic," which quickly outsold New Coke.

tions" that would affect only sixty random extra-inning games a year is hardly the way to keep the young in the ballpark or in front of their television sets—or, for that matter, in touch with the game for an extended length of time on any mobile screen. Reporters questioning Torre might also have pointed out that if an extra-inning game really is boring, a fan can simply leave the ballpark or turn off the television. Whether people stay for extra innings at the park or watch the *rara avis* fifteen- or sixteen-inning game on television, they are presumably doing so because the action is not dull but interesting.

I have interviewed both Rob Manfred and Tony Clark about the length and pacing of games, because if any changes are to be made that would shorten the game significantly (as opposed to shaving just a few minutes off each inning), these two men would probably have to agree on them at some point. As their comments in press conferences indicate, they have different views about whether baseball's traditional tempo is a serious liability in a Twitter world or a fundamental characteristic of the sport that ought to be tweaked with extreme caution. Manfred, born in 1958, is a Harvard-educated lawyer who has worked for Major League Baseball full-time since 1998 and was selected by the owners as commissioner in 2014. He had served as outside legal counsel to the owners during the disastrous 232-day strike of 1994–95, which resulted in the cancellation of the 1994 World Series. Many hefty books have been written about the strike, but there is near-unanimous agreement that it took the game years to recover from the wounds of a labor negotiation that deprived fans of the sport's traditional showcase.[19] Clark, born in 1972, had a fifteen-year career as a first baseman, but he missed the strike because he was not called up from the minor leagues until the labor dispute was settled in 1995. Clark was active as a union representative when he was a player and joined the players' association staff in 2010, shortly after his retirement from baseball. Since 2013, he has been the union's executive director. The two men share not only an obvious love of baseball and an interest in commonsensical solutions but a candor that is unusual at their level of a big business.

It is reasonable to assume that the thinking of both Clark and Manfred was shaped by the rancor of the strike—Clark because he began to play in the major leagues when the emotions of players were still raw, Manfred because he had provided legal advice to the equally angry owners. Since 1995, neither the owners nor the players' union has displayed an appetite for irreconcilable confrontation. The strike in the 1990s represented a grievous misjudgment; a second strike in the past two decades might have been a death blow as far as fans who remember 1994 are concerned. Whether they blamed the players or the owners, fans stayed away from the ballparks in droves in 1995, when attendance was down by 20 percent.[20] There are many in baseball who believe that there is an indirect, if not a direct, connection between the strike and the steroid era that followed. Before fans knew about the extent of performance-enhancing drug use in baseball, the steroid-fueled feats of Barry Bonds, Mark McGwire, and Sammy Sosa put many aggrieved fans back in the seats.

After the steroid scandal broke, producing another wave of fan disillusionment, labor peace became even more important. In 2002, Manfred and Donald Fehr, then head of the players' union, negotiated M.L.B.'s first drug-testing agreement. The era of labor peace in baseball has continued under Manfred and Clark. In the fall of 2016, after the spectacular (and spectacularly profitable) World Series between the Cubs and Indians, the players' union and M.L.B. reached a new collective bargaining agreement that does not expire until 2021.

Both men have reason to be equally concerned about the aging of baseball's fan base, but Manfred, unlike Clark, has argued that rule changes to speed up the pace within the game would make baseball more attractive to younger fans. In his interview with me (and in conversations reported by many sportswriters), he has proposed limits on the number of relief pitchers and the number of pitching changes within a game. The imposition of a pitcher's clock, as well as limiting the number of times a batter can step out of the batter's box and a pitcher can throw to first base, are also ideas that Manfred has backed and the union has resisted. There are obvious reasons why the union would resist some of these proposals; limiting the number of pitching changes, to cite one example, could mean that some middle relievers would lose their jobs. But most of the rule changes that Manfred supports have nothing to do with jobs and much more to do with his conviction that the pacing of the game itself is too slow for a generation raised from infancy on glowing screens.

Clark sounds like more of a traditionalist—at least about the pace of action within the game. I asked him specifically, since he was a first baseman, about the idea of limiting the number of times a pitcher could throw to first base. "You and Keith Hernandez would probably have had less back strain," I observed in a written question to Clark. "Seriously, though, wouldn't this sort of change erase a duel that isn't boring, but exciting, to watch? That is, it's exciting if a fan IS educated about the game. Can you think of anything that would shorten the game without turning it into something other than baseball?" Clark replied, "Agreed. The chess match that currently occurs would become more akin to a game of checkers and predictable if some of the considerations out there are implemented." Clark also mentioned the seldom-discussed issue (outside of baseball's inner circles) of player development in the minor leagues. "More development at the minor league levels . . . could help shorten games at the Major League level," he says, because "learning at the Major League level requires a lot of time, patience and hand holding . . . all of which affect the style, flow, length and quality of play."

Manfred, who speaks with great conviction about baseball being "a durable institution with a unique place in American life," is equally convinced that if M.L.B. ignores concerns about the slow pace of the game, it does so at its own peril.[21] "You just can't ignore what fans are telling you as if their choices were as limited as they were fifty years ago," he says. Most of the complaints, though, come from fans watching the game on television rather than fans in the ballpark. That makes perfect sense on one level. All ballparks that have opened or been thoroughly renovated since the late 1990s have as much in common with amusement parks, shopping malls, and restaurant-filled blocks as they do with the older parks that offered only . . . well, baseball.

Chase Field, the home of the Arizona Diamondbacks in Phoenix, has not only a swimming pool but a hot tub behind the right-field fence. Tropicana Field in Tampa has a "touch tank," where people can actually touch live rays swimming around. The Mets' Citi Field, which opened in 2009 and replaced grungy Shea Stadium (which inspired every Mets fan's motto, "It's a dump, but it's *our* dump"), has stores and restaurants galore, at various price levels. A fan who is bored with a low-scoring game can relieve his or her ennui (although a reservation is usually needed) at an establishment owned by upscale New York restaurateur Drew Nieporent, for a prix fixe of $33.* The less well-heeled may stand in line at dozens of establishments, ranging from kosher hot dog stands to Danny Meyer's Shake Shack. In these lines, where it usually takes at least an inning to acquire food, you may watch the action on the field on your own iPhone (if you have the right app) or the ballpark's television screens. So it isn't surprising that the game seems shorter and quicker to many fans in a ballpark than at home.

What is odd is that television watchers would voice more complaints about the game's slow pace. People who watch games on television are not chained to their couches any more than people are chained to their seats in the ballpark. I feel safe in saying that

*By the time you read this book, the price will probably have gone up.

almost no one in a noncomatose state sits and watches a game on television for three or more solid hours, unless it's a game with the sustained tension of the decisive Astros-Mets contest in 1986. Like many fans, I am not even aware of the length of commercial breaks because I never watch commercials. The only Mets' sponsor I can name is Citibank, and that is only because the ballpark is called Citi Field. ("Our dump," by contrast, was named for a real human being—Bill Shea, a wheeling and dealing New York lawyer who was the person most responsible for bringing National League baseball back to New York after the city's abandonment by the Dodgers and Giants.) In any case, I use commercials to cook, do the dishes, take a shower, make a stab at straightening up my home office for the next day. When the game itself is truly boring—say, when one team scores ten runs in the first two innings—I engage in all of the activities that are usually reserved for commercials. Sometimes I try to clean up the living room instead of my office, in the unlikely event of a comeback.

I am not convinced that anyone in baseball truly believes that cutting the game back a full hour (a near-impossibility, even if anyone had the slightest intention of cutting the length and number of commercials) would eliminate the challenge baseball faces in its effort to attract and keep a younger fan base. The real cloud, much bigger than a man's hand, that looms over the future of this prosperous sport is the diminution of concentration —a phenomenon affecting Americans of all ages. Here is the most ominous statistic from Nielsen in 2017: since 2014, there has been a 15 percent decrease in the number of categories in which people say they are "intensely" interested and a 15 percent increase in categories (including all measurable forms of entertainment) in which people are "slightly" interested.[22] "Slightly," for a game as demanding as baseball, just isn't good enough.

5 the "national pastime" and the national culture of distraction

Don't you know how hard this all is?

—TED WILLIAMS

Here is the fan baseball must cultivate today if the game hopes to preserve its special place in the American imagination into the 2040s. I will not speculate about later decades, when the game will be two centuries old. For all I know, the 2050s and 2060s will see a technological revolution as profound and destabilizing to established institutions as the digital revolution we are still navigating in the second decade of the twenty-first century. Let us say that our hypothetical post-millennial child is about twelve years old—the age when many boys and girls, unless they have displayed exceptional athletic ability, cut way back on their active involvement in sports.

This future baseball fan (or not) was born in 2006—a year that may one day be considered a turning point in the media drive for total penetration of the human market. In early 2006, the pretentious Baby Einstein series of videos aimed at toddlers whose parents were already grooming them for the Ivy League was joined by the first television channel, BabyFirstTV, aimed not at sophisticated two- and three-year-olds but at infants in the cradle. BabyFirst, now available on every type of screen, marketed itself as commercial-free, but the entire project might properly be described as a commercial for television itself (as well as for all types of screens). This commercial begins before the target audience is physically and mentally capable of turning the program off or making an advertisement disappear. So, our twelve-year-old may well have had a screen over his bed before he was weaned.* By age five, according to a report released in 2011 by Common Sense Media, half of all children in this age group had a television set in their bedrooms. And half of children under eight had access to a mobile device, such as an iPad or iPhone.[1] From Day One, this child has been soothed, excited, and captivated by all of the products offered by the mass media.

Today our twelve-year-old middle school student spends roughly four and a half hours a day watching television—an increase of about forty minutes since 2004. This does not mean that he is watching programs specifically created for television but that he is sampling all of the wares that can now be streamed on any screen. He spends only thirty-eight minutes (give or take a few) reading each day—down five minutes between 2004 and 2009.† He also spends at least an hour and a quarter on video games, and another two and a half hours on music and audio programs (whether on the computer or the iPhone, we do not

*Throughout the rest of this chapter, I will use the generic "he," as I have used the generic "she" in other parts of the book, for the sake of convenience. I have chosen the generic "he" in this instance because boys consume much more digital media than girls do.

†All of these statistics are from the Kaiser Family Foundation's most recent report, published in 2010. No other studies of children's media consumption are as comprehensive, although results from more recent surveys by the Pew Research Center, and from Nielsen, indicate that the time devoted to digital media consumption has only increased since 2010.

know). Time spent on video games more than doubled in the eight-to-eighteen age group between 2004 and 2009. The video game industry itself is a growing behemoth, earning more than $30.4 billion in revenue in the United States alone in 2016.[2]

Twelve is also the age at which many children—especially boys—become fans of e-sports. E-sports are not to be confused with fantasy sports (their impact on baseball will be discussed later), whose participants form mythical sports teams and select their players based on the vast pool of readily available statistics in the era of digital sabermetrics. E-sports, by contrast, are simply elaborate video games, and 51 percent of boys (but only 20 percent of girls) ages twelve to nineteen report watching these competitions online or even streamed on big screens in sporting venues. A report by Project Play—an Aspen Institute–sponsored program designed to encourage children's participation in active sports—contends that although e-sports are *marketed* as "sports," they are not really sports because "there is little or no physical activity involved."[3] Thus e-sports—like the gross and all-too-real Nathan's Famous annual hot dog eating contests held every Fourth of July at Coney Island—should properly be called competitions. In recent years, media companies and advertisers have participated in the branding of video game competitions as sports because so many young people are now watching.

The use of all types of media, according to the American Psychological Association, increases most dramatically among children from ages eleven to fourteen.[4] Overall, total reported media use in the eight-to-eighteen age group rose by more than 18 percent between 2004 and 2010. For both children and young adults, total media consumption is the most relevant figure, and it has gone up substantially since 2010, even though young adults are viewing content more on mobile devices and less on traditional television sets. At the beginning of 2017, Nielsen reported that media consumption on smartphones had surpassed television for the first time among adults ages eighteen to thirty-four.[5]

These were the numbers on M.L.B. Commissioner Rob Manfred's mind when he talked about the wide array of choices available to young teenagers—soon to be young adults glued to their smartphones—who might have been faithful baseball fans a half-century ago (or even thirty years ago, before mobile devices and before most homes had personal computers). These are the young fans whom the players' union head Tony Clark wants to educate about the game even though that education does not come as naturally today as it did in his generation, let alone for generations of fans now in their fifties and sixties.

I have concluded, after interviewing at least one hundred young adults in their late teens and twenties for this book, that all of the current statistics about media consumption by post-millennial children as well as by the millennial generation are vastly understated. (My selection of interviewees was not "scientific"; when I spoke at colleges during the past few years, I asked students who were willing to be interviewed about the subject to contact me. However, much of what they told me did support the conclusions of studies by professional polling organizations, such as the Pew Forum, on the subject of media use.) There is simply no way, given the adeptness of the young at multitasking by using various digital devices simultaneously, to measure the number of hours they really spend online—much less the impact on their attention spans. Most of the high school and college students I interviewed about this subject did not want me to use their real names. When I asked why, they would usually admit that they did not want their parents and teachers to know how much time they spent on social media (girls) or playing video games (boys). According to a Pew Research Center online survey, 24 percent of teens say they go online "almost constantly" on their smartphones, 56 percent "several times a day," and 92 percent at least once a day.[6] "They're lying," said a sixteen-year-old Manhattan high school junior whom I will call Meryl. "I don't know what 'constantly' means, but my friends and I are on Facebook or Snapchat every ten minutes. The only time I'm not checking my phone that often is in class, where there are rules against it. And there are teachers who will see that your phone gets taken away for the rest of the day if you get caught." Meryl, as it happens, considers herself a baseball fan (she follows the standings on her phone) and a Mets fan, but she accepts her parents' invitations to go to the ballpark with them only twice a season. "It just takes too much time," she said. I asked her whether she took her smartphone to the ballpark. "Oh, sure," she replied, "but it makes my dad crazy, so a lot of the time I'll get up and say I have to go to the bathroom so I can go and check my texts without getting hassled." This is a succinct summation of the mindset of a casual young fan who might either lose interest in baseball altogether as she grows up or turn into a mother who encourages her children to play. Transforming a teenager like Meryl into an adult who continues to be interested in baseball and introduces her children to the game may be the most difficult task M.L.B. and the players face today. She is now a multimedia and multisports consumer rather than someone for whom baseball has an emotional meaning worth an extended investment of time. When she actually goes to a ballgame today, she is there but not all there.

Whatever the precise amount of time eight-to-eighteen-year-olds spend online, all surveys of children's media consumption provide an important backdrop for Nielsen's 2017 finding that fewer adults are "intensely interested" in one subject or pastime, while many more are apt to be "slightly interested" in several categories. The virtual world's business is distraction. You may be annoyed when an advertisement for olive oil (you took a trip to Italy last year) pops up and blocks whatever you are trying to read online, but many consumers are delighted. Olive oil may well be more interesting than whatever you were trying to find out in the first place. Distraction leads naturally to dilution of interest, whether one is watching a sporting event, listening to music, or doing research for a homework paper.

I asked all of the teenagers I interviewed whether they would be more likely to pay attention to a game that lasted two instead of three hours. They all shook their heads and laughed. "I don't do anything except homework for more than an hour at a time," said Meryl's eighteen-year-old boyfriend Josh (his name has also been changed). The percentage of a day spent on electronic media by teenagers is the elephant, or hopping kangaroo, in the room for both baseball and reading as "pastimes"—national or otherwise. If the studies are right, most teenagers spend roughly eight hours a day checking out one screen or another. School, if you are talking about a day that begins around eight with a trip in a bus or car and ends around three, takes up another seven hours. That leaves exactly nine hours for homework (of which there is a staggering amount in comparison with the homework assigned to previous generations), eating, seeing other people (including family) face to face, and sleeping. Not much time for reading or anything else. Weekends are a possibility, of course, but kids would have to want to make baseball (or reading, for that matter) a priority. Meryl and Josh, on their most recent Saturday night date, had spent the evening with friends binge-watching streamed episodes of season 2 of the American Movie Classics series *Better Call Saul.*

It is easy to understand why anyone who talks about the conflict between baseball's traditional culture of concentration and a modern market that sells interruption could be accused of being as shortsighted as the baseball owners who feared radio in the 1920s and television in the early 1950s. There is, however, a fundamental difference between the two earlier media shifts—the first to radio and the second to television—and the digital revolution (and not only with regard to baseball). Radio—with the exception of car radios—and television were not portable and available twenty-four hours a day. While these media offered new forms of entertainment, they did not easily or automatically supplant the old ones.

The owners who originally thought that radio would reduce attendance at major league games seemed oblivious to the fact that for most Americans working in cities in the 1920s, going to a game during the week was impossible. For Americans who did not live in or near major league cities, baseball at the highest level was simply out of reach at any time. People who lived in the Blue Ridge mountains of Virginia during the Depression, even in the unlikely event that they had access to an automobile, were not about to spend money on gas to drive to Washington, D.C., to see the Senators play. Yes, there were trains—but an ordinary visitor would have had to stay with family or friends, since paying for a hotel was an unthinkable luxury at the time. What radio did was bring ballgames into the homes and town public spaces of people who otherwise would not have been able to attend big-league games. The number of radios in homes increased from 12 million in 1929 to more than 28 million in 1939.[7] One frequently overlooked aspect of the broadcasting of baseball on radio was that it attracted a new group of female fans, who were more likely than men to be at home during the day. Look at early-twentieth-century film of ballpark crowds in the 1994 Ken Burns series *Baseball,* first aired on the Public Broadcasting Service, and you see that the fans were nearly all men. Radio changed that. Women who might have seen baseball played only on the schoolyard or on the Fourth of July could imagine the professional game as announcers followed it play by play. My grandmother, who grew up in a poor family in Chicago in the first two decades of the twentieth century—when girls did not go to the ballpark even if they had the price of admission— became a real fan only when she started listening to the game on radio in the 1920s. There is no question that radio, rather than discouraging people from going to the ballpark, encouraged those who had never thought of seeing a game live before. "Your Gramps had already been to ballgames, both the White Sox and the Cubs," my grandmother told me, "but I never thought of going. The first time I heard a game on the radio while I was doing my ironing, I asked him to take me the next time he went. He said, 'Why, Min, I'm an idiot never to have taken you. You'll love it.' And I did. You could only go with your husband or father or brother, though. It wasn't considered nice for women to go just with other girlfriends." In the 1950s, when I was learning baseball while watching television in my grandfather's bar, my grandmother would bring trays of sandwiches for everyone and spend the afternoon, as I did, watching the game with the men. We were not watching on television because we preferred the bar to the ballpark; we were simply following the game on a day when none of us would have gone out to the park anyway. The following Saturday, some of us might well watch a game not on television but from the stands of Comiskey Park or Wrigley Field.

Mobile devices, by contrast, are used by people who, like Meryl and her boyfriend, really do not want to devote hours to any sport (or, in many instances, to the other varied forms of entertainment available on iPhones and iPads). The media consumption habits of the millennial and postmillennial generations today are fundamentally at odds with the suspension of time that has always been part of baseball's distinctive charm. After speaking with many teenagers who told me that watching the same game for two hours was as sluggish an experience as watching for three hours, I do not think M.L.B. can institute any rule changes that would make real inroads into the shortened attention span of the young without fundamentally altering the game. What if you did end every extra-inning game with a home run derby, or shorten at-bats by making a third foul ball a strikeout? (Manfred, I should emphasize, has made no such radical proposals.) Changing the foul ball rule—a suggestion that frequently pops up on sports Web sites—would change the rigor and exactitude of the game into something entirely different, but it would not shorten the game enough to make younger fans delight in watching baseball as it was meant to be played. In contrast to the reaction of owners in the early days of radio and television, M.L.B. has tended to take a "if you can't beat 'em, join 'em" attitude toward digital technology—trying to treat it as an adjunct to the game rather than a competitor. Under Manfred, M.L.B. had upgraded its streaming capabilities, and the Disney Company was so impressed that in 2016, it announced the investment of $1 billion in baseball's advanced technology unit. Baseball offers streaming packages on MLB.tv as well as its popular At Bat app, which provides scores, statistics, and the audio of games for only $2.99 a month.

Tony Clark also has ideas about using technology to attract younger fans. Asked how baseball can respond to the competition for young people's attention that did not exist forty years ago, Clark replied, "I think one of the ways is to implement currently available technology to provide varied broadcast options." As an example, he proposed that viewers might decide whether they want to listen to a broadcast dominated by coverage of pitching or hitting. "Presently your options are limited despite the great job that a number of broadcast outlets and play-by-play analysts do," he says. "Whether you are a new fan to the game or a seasoned fan, there would seem to be a benefit to being able to further break down the finer points of the game to establish a foundation of understanding."[8] I was slightly appalled by this suggestion at first, because it seemed antithetical to the ideal experience of a baseball game as a unified entity. Was the great 1986 playoff game between the Mets and the Astros a hitter's game or a pitcher's game? Of course, it was both, and a good announcer is able to comment on both. On the other hand, one thing that makes an exceptional game exceptional, and an ordinary game ordinary, is that the exceptional game usually involves a continual tension-filled balance between pitching and hitting. In an ordinary game, assuming the presence of halfway decent pitchers on the mound, I am more interested in pitching than in hitting. I would probably like to try out a broadcast in which special emphasis is placed on pitching. But I'm not at all sure that this interest would be shared by a young fan who does not fully understand the game. I have visions of teenagers switching broadcasts constantly on their smartphones and trying to find wherever the action is. Whether that would be a bad, good, or neutral thing, it would satisfy the need for a continuous change of scenery and subject. You could create your own fantasy of baseball, with the audio equivalent of a split screen, instead of watching the game as it unfolds before you, at its own pace and beyond your control.

The relationship of fantasy baseball to real baseball is much more complicated than the straightforward competition for attention provided by other online activities. There are basically two groups of fantasy sports fans—those who join with friends, without any significant prizes or gambling, for the fun of pitting their wits and their fictional rosters against one another's, and those involved in commercially sponsored leagues that encourage and make money from gambling. Commercial fantasy sports are not, at least in theory, for children; most states have laws forbidding anyone under eighteen from registering on the sites. But people under eighteen do play fantasy sports online, and, given the tenuous nature of authentication of identity for any activity on the Internet, that is hardly surprising. I met two high school students, both boys, who not only played both baseball and football online but frequently placed bets of more than $100 on their fantasy teams. (They were both from well-off families and had saved money from birthday presents to finance their habit.) Keeping knowledge of this activity from the parents was one reason they did not want to be identified when asked how much time they spent online. Regardless of whether young teenagers participate in fantasy sports themselves, they are being shaped by this now-digital business.

All fantasy sports today are heirs to what was once called Rotisserie Baseball, founded by the writer Daniel Okrent—whose subjects range from baseball to Prohibition—in 1980. The game was named for a restaurant, La Rotisserie Française, that used to be located on East 52nd Street in Manhattan. While having lunch at the restaurant in winter, Okrent and a group of friends worked out the rules for "drafting" players, based on statistics then available only in each day's box scores in the newspapers. It should be said that a fantasy game of this kind is probably better suited to baseball than any other sport, if only because baseball has the longest history of record keeping. Also, most serious baseball fans are, in some sense, statistics nerds. Long before there were organized fantasy sports, many true baseball fans devoted a scandalous amount of time to thinking about how much better a job they could do of managing or owning a baseball team than the people who actually owned or managed teams. This syndrome, which I sometimes think belongs in the American Psychiatric Association's Diagnostic and Statistical Manual of Mental Disorders, is particularly evident in fans of hard-luck teams. At the beginning of the 2017 season, for instance, I was convinced that the Mets were going nowhere because they were counting on young starting pitchers who had already been injured several times in their minor league and major league careers, several of whom had undergone major surgery or been on the disabled list the previous season. Sure enough, as I write in mid-June, four of the five young men who were supposed to be the top Mets' starters are on the disabled list. I would have taken that into account if I were assembling a team for fantasy baseball. I would have assembled a better team by factoring the long-term impact of early injuries into my acquisitions last winter. Why didn't the Mets' general manager Sandy Alderson do so? I've always thought that Okrent's status as a Cubs fan was one of the reasons he was able to dream up Rotisserie Baseball in 1980. At that time, the Cubs' drought still had thirty-six years to go. In fantasy baseball, you can insert an element of your own skill—the knowledge acquired over decades of watching the game and studying the numbers—to achieve a winning outcome.

According to the Fantasy Sports Trade Association (the oxy-moronic wackiness of this title is revealing), more than 57 million people—two-thirds of them men—played in some type of fantasy league in 2015. The association claims that more than half are college educated and have annual incomes over $75,000.[9] What Okrent could not have anticipated when he and his friends casually set up their Rotisserie League in 1980 was the explosion of possibilities and interest that would be created by personal computers. In 1980, you either had to wait for the printed box scores to make your "management" decisions or, if you were a true addict and had access to a newspaper or television network office, you could skulk around a behemoth telex and get the latest results from cities three time zones away. What began as winter recreation for friendly baseball geeks (or geeky baseball friends) has now turned into a business in which gambling plays as important a role as interest in the game.

Nevertheless, there are still two different groups among fantasy baseball enthusiasts today—those for whom camaraderie and intellectual competition are paramount, and those who are, deep down, sports gamblers. In the first group, friends get together mainly to keep in touch with one another and with the game, in a competition that requires regular contact. Prizes are small and side bets are rarely more than $10. Thirty-year-old Daniel, an economist for a think tank in southern California (both his name and occupation have been changed), has played for five years in two leagues started by close friends—some of whom met in high school and others in graduate school. Daniel's league does not play in the off season. He estimates that during the season, he and his friends play once a week in contests that last about an hour and a half. Before the "draft," Daniel says he does four to eight hours of statistical research in order to select the players he wants for his team. "If you want to be a 'statsy fan,' it's a lot easier now," he says. "I think the fantasy today is more about being a general manager of a team rather than a manager, because it's the general manager who gets to do trades. It's a fantasy of control."

Fantasy baseball is also a socially acceptable way for men to keep in touch with one another. "We underestimate the amount of time we spend on all of this," says twenty-eight-year-old Bill, a New York advertising executive whose name and profession have also been changed. "There's a lot of texting back and forth about trades that I don't count when I say I only spend about two hours a week on it in the summer. It's probably more like five. And that doesn't count the fights I have with my girlfriend about the time I spend on it. She thinks it's not teenage stuff, but, as she puts it, 'middle school stuff.' And truthfully, I have been playing fantasy baseball, just with friends and not for real money, since I was thirteen. We did a lot of talking about girls back then. My girlfriend says we should just go to a ballgame, but that's different. Even if going to one game a week would take no more time than I now spend online, it *feels* longer. It's hard to explain."

If you want to know why fantasy players do not want to use their real names, the explanation may be no more complicated than fear that older bosses would have the same attitude toward fantasy sports as Bill's girlfriend—that they're somewhat childish. When I interviewed fantasy baseball players in their twenties and early thirties—all of them volunteers—I found that they were as reluctant to be identified in print as were teenagers scared that their parents would find out about their sports gambling. Brendan Dwyer, a researcher at the Center for Sport Leadership at Virginia Commonwealth University (his real name and occupation), has described fantasy sports as "the male version of a book club."[10] Several of the men I interviewed used the same analogy, but all were players who did not do any high-stakes gambling. For some of these men, it is possible that being known as a participant in the male version of a book club would embarrass them more than being known as a gambler.

Although the Fantasy Sports Trade Association claims that a third of all players are women, that proportion is probably much smaller in fantasy baseball leagues. Most of the men I interviewed said that their leagues had had female players at various times, but the women tended to drop out. This may reflect baseball's relatively smaller female fan base in the real, as distinct from the virtual, world. It may also mean simply that baseball-loving women between ages eighteen and thirty-four (the age group with the largest number of fantasy sports participants) are far too busy—especially if they have children—to spend time texting each other about what a just-reported thumb injury to a starting pitcher means to their prospects.

For the group of non–book club fantasy sports players interested mainly in gambling (or as much in gambling as they are in sport), the stakes are obviously different. To enter leagues and compete with fictitious rosters, participants pay an entry fee to companies, such as FanDuel and DraftKings, which pay out millions in weekly cash prizes. This is not the statsy fan pastime envisaged by the group at La Rotisserie Française, and it does not represent the sort of low-stakes conviviality that characterizes Daniel's and Bill's leagues. It's big business, and professional sports, including M.L.B., are heavily invested in it. The reason: fantasy sports players, particularly those who play nearly every day on commercial sites like FanDuel, watch 40 percent more games on television and other screens once they start participating in the virtual world of sports.[11] People who bet significant sums on fantasy sports are obviously more likely than others to watch a televised game, and watch it to the end, because if a player on a fictional fantasy team does well in the real game, the fantasy player has a better chance of winning and taking home a money prize. (Remember: in fantasy sports, statistical performance, and therefore winning or losing, is based on the shifting statistics of athletes on real playing fields.)

Let us say that the faux "general manager" of a fantasy baseball team lives in Kansas City. He is not rooting for the Kansas City Royals to beat the New York Yankees in reality on a given day, but for "his" players to do well in the real world so that the faux general manager can win in the virtual world. If the fantasy general manager picked the Yankees' spectacular rookie Aaron Judge for his team before the beginning of the 2017 season, he was probably on a high during the early part of that spring. In 2015, M.L.B. signed a partnership agreement with DraftKings, the chief rival of FanDuel, making the former the "Official Daily Fantasy Game" of Major League Baseball. Funny, I always thought that the daily fantasy game of baseball was what was going on in my head.

One particularly tawdry aspect of the relationship between sports and commercial fantasy enterprises is the pretense that somehow, fantasy sports really have nothing to do with gambling and are pure games of skill. In 2016, the New York State Legislature passed a bill rejecting the opinion of State Attorney General Eric Schneiderman, who found that fantasy sports were games of chance and therefore illegal under New York state law. Governor Andrew Cuomo signed the bill into law with a pious statement about providing supervision and protection for participants. Prizes awarded by DraftKings and FanDuel would, of course, bring the state new tax revenue. State Assemblyman J. Gary Pretlow, unlike Cuomo, was blunt about the motivation. "Fantasy sports are more than online games," he said. "They have the potential to generate millions of dollars in revenue for New York State."[12] Sandra Rayme, a vice president of the American Gaming Association, described Daily Fantasy Sports as "the gift that keeps on giving—it's mainstreamed our business."[13] She said this with pride, not shame.

The role of gambling in commercially sponsored fantasy sports is underlined for me by my interviews with off-the-grid fantasy players like Bill and Daniel, who generally shun games on television and who have a somewhat superior attitude toward those who do watch. Most of these men told me they go weeks at a time without ever turning on a game on television or any other screen. Sports, either real or virtual, are not their entire life, and baseball is not apt to make any money from them by investing in fantasy sports. They haven't placed any large bets on their imaginary teams, so they have no reason to turn on the television and keep up, minute by minute, with the performance of "their" players. There are exceptions to this general rule; the fantasy sports world is filled with people who write, read, and breathe sports for a variety of reasons that seem to have nothing to do with gambling or with the desire for the equivalent of book club buddies. The Web site Rotowire.com offers invaluable insights into the minds of the obsessed fan. Renee Miller, a neuroscientist at the University of Rochester and the author of a 2013 e-book titled *Cognitive Bias in Fantasy Sports: Is Your Brain Sabotaging Your Team?,* plays fantasy football, basketball, and baseball—and she watches all three sports on television as well. Miller is a serious scientist, but her thoughts about the "greater variability" of outcomes in baseball than in football or basketball are comical to read. In a passage that evokes some of the same responses in a reader as postmodernist philosophy does in most college freshmen, she writes:

> Baseball DFS [daily fantasy sports] turned me on to a level of sports variability that I had never experienced before. I've written about it here so many times. The range of outcomes for even the best players just blows me away. . . . A baseball DFS lineup is just as likely to withstand four Ks from Mike Trout and cash, as have Anthony Rizzo hit two home runs and not cash, while the difference between Kevin Durant scoring 40 or 60 FPTs will almost certainly affect the outcome of your N.B.A. cash games. N.F.L. falls somewhere in the middle, with a wider range of outcomes than M.L.B., but each one mattering a lot like N.B.A. It makes it fun for me that there isn't one "solution" to DFS strategy.[14]

It's hard to understand why anyone would be "blown away" by the ability of a good lineup to overcome a bad performance by a great individual player. (By the way, "cash" is just fantasy sports jargon for winning in a particular kind of fantasy baseball game. For the fine points, see www.rotowire.com or any other fantasy sports Web site with a glossary of technical terminology.) The greater variability, or unpredictability, of baseball outcomes is inevitable when every batter is entitled to three strikes and every team must get three outs in an inning. Of course Mike Trout, the star center fielder (in real baseball) for the Los Angeles Angels, can strike out four times and his team can still come away with a win. Of course the same would be true of a fantasy team that included Trout. There are eight other hitters who all get *their* three swings. And of course if Kevin Durant, the great forward for the Golden State Warriors, scores 60 points in a real N.B.A. game, it will be hard to beat the Warriors unless no one else on their team does any scoring. In a fantasy game, the same would be true. When players can never sit on their hands and wait for the buzzer to end the game, bad individual performances can be overcome.

There is little doubt, from reading commentary by devout fantasy players, that participants in the current commercial iteration of Rotisserie ball are more likely to consume more sports on various media. The long-term effects on baseball cannot be predicted at this point. Although the business of fantasy baseball is very much at ease with the business of baseball, it may be very much at odds with baseball as a game. There is something distasteful about trying to attract younger fans—remember, today's twelve-year-olds will be old enough to legally deal themselves into online sports in 2024—by something other than the real game.

Okrent, by the way, gave up fantasy baseball in 2009. (Full disclosure: we met and have both worked in the Allen Room, a haven for nonfiction writers in the New York Public Library.) Since then, he says, he has become a more active fan, taking joy in the game itself, rooting for the Cubs, and finally being rewarded in 2016. Could there be any greater fulfillment of a fan's fantasy?

Returning to those twelve-year-olds, I would be remiss not to acknowledge that M.L.B. is making a real attempt to address the most serious obstacle to the development of young fans— the fact that fewer children and teenagers play baseball or softball than in the past. The best that can be said about expanding M.L.B.'s digital scope is that kids will be able to check in on baseball, if they are so inclined, as they access snippets of other sports, concerts, and video games. But there is no reliable evidence—zilch, nada, bupkes—that online activities, including forays into fantasy baseball at an early age, can create a real fan who goes to the ballpark and follows the game and its star athletes for the sheer fun of it.

Because there is considerable evidence that adult fans are formed in childhood, by playing or being exposed to some form of baseball or softball, it is especially disturbing that all youth sports—and physical activity in general—have been in decline in the United States for at least two decades. One of Manfred's most interesting interviews since becoming M.L.B.

commissioner was conducted not by a grizzled sportswriter but by a teenage reporter, Amiri Tulloch, for *Sports Illustrated Kids*. Tulloch asked Manfred an astute question: "Are you interested in getting kids to play baseball or just watch it?" Manfred replied, "Both. It is important for our sport that kids play because that gets them interested in the game and they're more likely to be fans. But it's also important to get them in the ballpark. Our ballpark experience is a family-friendly experience that the sooner a young person engages in it, the more likely he is to be a fan for his whole life." Indeed, M.L.B.'s research indicates that the age a child was when a parent first took him to the ballpark is almost as important in creating adult fans as having played ball as a child.[15]

The play does not have to be highly organized, highly competitive, or driven by adult pressure to occupy an important role in the psyches of children. I'm proof of that. I was—I did not want to admit this in the first chapter—*always* the proverbial last kid chosen. Yes, the other girls as well as the boys were better, particularly in the field, than I was. I was afraid of every ball hit sharply (even by grade school standards) toward me. One might think I would have hated the game because of my own ineptitude, but playing had the opposite effect: what I learned was how much skill and training it must take to accomplish as simple-*appearing* a professional baseball move as catching a grounder to shortstop and throwing it to first base in time to get the runner out. I'm not sure if I hadn't had the experience of playing baseball at play that my baseball education in my grandfather's bar would have embedded itself so thoroughly in my memory.

In any case, both semisupervised play at recess and unsupervised play outdoors have almost disappeared from American life, and there is no bringing old-fashioned childhood back. In a security-conscious world, many parents are happy (despite the many dangers on the Internet) to have their kids staring at iPad or iPhone screens in their bedrooms. They know where their kids are; they just don't know where their kids' minds are. As for public education, the emphasis on frequent and early standardized testing since 2000 has led many schools to cut back on or eliminate recess time altogether. State budget cuts—and, again, the immense stress surrounding standardized testing—have persuaded some school districts to eliminate physical education in high school altogether. In 2016, SHAPE America (the Society of Health and Physical Educators) released a survey indicating that schools receive an average of $764 a year (not per pupil but per school) for exercise programs. The $764 does not include teacher salaries—only unimportant things like equipment, from volleyballs to baseball bats, and maintenance for safety purposes. Just one state—Oregon—and the District of Columbia offer physical education programs that meet guidelines set by the American Heart Association.[16]

Therein lies the importance of the Play Ball youth initiative, sponsored by M.L.B. and USA Baseball (the governing body of amateur baseball). Play Ball is attempting to draw more kids into enjoying games with balls and sticks—whether as part of an organized league or as the brainchild of a parent who simply wants his or her children and their friends to get more exercise. On the Play Ball Web site, parents and children can find a variety of resources, including the free Play Ball mobile coaching app for Android devices. M.L.B. has invested more than $30 million to introduce Play Ball in 140 cities. "It's great to see that they're emphasizing cheaper alternatives for kids to play," said Nancy Maxwell, a coach in the Bronx.[17]

"Cheaper" is the key word here. Today's twelve-year-old is only one year away from the point at which 70 percent of American children drop out of organized sports altogether, according to the National Alliance for Sports. The cost of sports to kids who do continue with organized play after middle school—and to their parents—can be staggering. In baseball, a minimum of $2,000 for travel costs, equipment, and specialized coaching is the rule rather than the exception. Many middle-class parents, whatever their race, have no choice but to say no. Given the cost of college, what sensible parent would not want to save that money to reduce his or her child's future student loan debt? The 2016 Project Play report provides stark evidence of just how well off a family has to be to enter the elite, semiprofessionalized world of elite teenage sports. In 2015, only 38 percent of teens from families with an income of $25,000 or less played team sports, compared with 67 percent of those from homes with more than $100,000 in household income.[18] Given that the median income of American families is around $51,000, that statistic tells you all you need to know about why so many teens drop out of sports.

The cost of specialized training at an early age affects all sports, but baseball is particularly vulnerable because of the length of time needed to acquire the game's most sophisticated skills. When I was growing up, Little League—while its participants were the best players from local schools—was not costly. It was always sponsored by some small local business, and "traveling" meant, at most, driving forty-five minutes to an adjacent county. The coach was usually someone you knew—perhaps a high school phys ed teacher or a middle-aged neighbor who, it was rumored, had once played in the low minor leagues. The pressure and expense associated with baseball for teenagers is sadly congruent with the income inequality that is the defining political issue in the United States today. That M.L.B. has recognized the problem and is trying to put some of the "play" back in "play ball" is to its credit. The problem, inseparable from economic and class inequality, is both bigger than and an integral part of baseball.

conclusion: the reims baseball club:
why baseball matters

Baseball is the belly-button of our society. Straighten out baseball, you'll straighten out the rest of the world.

—BILL "SPACEMAN" LEE

The year was 1987, and I had overdosed on European culture on a Sunday afternoon in Reims, in the heart of France's champagne-producing region. Late in the afternoon, Luke and I had taken a tour of the city's famed thirteenth-century cathedral, in an effort to work off a spectacular four-course midday meal, consumed at an equally famous restaurant and accompanied, of course, by fine champagne. The cathedral cure didn't work; we were both suffering from a bad case of Stendhal syndrome, a combination of nausea and sensory overload brought on, in our case, by too much fine food and drink as well as too much beauty. We needed to sit down. We needed coffee—the stronger the better.

A five-minute walk from the cathedral, we came across a scruffy café with an intriguing small sign proclaiming that this was the headquarters of "The Reims Baseball Club." Surely this must be a mistake. We had no idea that anyone, anywhere in France was even remotely aware of American baseball. When we opened the door, we saw walls covered with posters of the New York Mets—Dwight Gooden, Keith Hernandez, and Darryl Strawberry most prominent among them. Strawberry's lanky image loomed over the espresso machine. Most of the café's customers were young men of roughly the same age as Gooden and Strawberry, and we immediately asked them to explain what the Reims Baseball Club was and how it came to be. There were a few English-speakers in the group, and Luke spoke fluent French, so communication was easy. These young Frenchmen had become fans of American baseball because two of their relatives—cousins or brothers, I don't remember which—had attended graduate school in New York and fallen in love with "our" national pastime. They became Mets fans, because the Mets at that point in New York's baseball history were a more exciting team than the Yankees. They learned to play with college friends in pickup games. When the Reims baseball fans came home on vacation, they brought VCR tapes of Mets games and explained baseball to their friends. This was, of course, just before personal computers conquered the world and the Internet provided universal access to baseball statistics and images. But the VCR tapes were enough to hook these particular young men of Reims on American baseball. When they learned that we had actually seen the Mets play, they would not let us leave and the owner would not accept our money for the espressos we downed. "Baseball is the most beautiful game I have ever seen," said one man. "And it ought to be perfect for France, because it's *très logique* (very logical). It will be popular in France someday. *Absolument*." Having followed Gooden in 1985 and 1986, the baseball club members were filled with sorrow at news, which surfaced publicly in 1987, of his problems with cocaine. How was he doing, they asked us—as if we knew him personally. What sort of *désintox* (rehab) was he undergoing? When we said their guess was as good as ours, they sighed. "Yes, it's always a mistake to think that sports heroes are gods," said one of the youngest men, who was learning to pitch from an American exchange student. Then he added, "If I were an American, I would be proud to be of the country that invented this game."

When Luke and I left the café, completely cured of artshock and our hangovers, we looked at each other with amazement and mild embarrassment. Since the Vietnam War, which had ended twelve years earlier, neither of us had felt especially proud to be an American when we were abroad. Viewed by our new Reims friends as exporters of the *double jeu* (double play) rather than napalm, we felt more American, in the best patriotic sense, than we had in years—as if, somehow, we were personally responsible for showing (even showing off) our country's better side. How good it felt to be seen as representatives of an America that had produced something *logique* rather then *illogique!* That young man, who was a philosophy student at the Sorbonne, had grasped something essential about baseball—that its appeal is grounded in logic and proportionality as well as beauty.

The Reims Baseball Club still exists. Its Web site informs readers, as our café informants had told us, that the club was founded in 1986 by "a few enthusiasts." (There is no mention of the Mets-mania of some of the early members.) Today, the club has participants from ages nine to fifteen at the junior level and sixteen to seventy-seven in the senior division. Women of all ages are also welcome. The senior team plays matches against other small French clubs from towns such as Nancy, Strasbourg, and Metz. It is pleasing to me to know that in corners of some small cities in France, on fine summer days, games are being played that will be forever America. Or, in any event, that will reflect the better angels of America's nature.

Leaving aside the question of whether baseball still merits the label of "national pastime," the game's historical identification with American patriotism has always incorporated some of the worst as well as the best elements of American exceptionalism. But that, too, is a part of what gives baseball its special place in both American iconography and American reality.

I could not agree more strongly with Bill Lee, whose natural sinkerball is dwarfed in baseball memory by his natural inability to utter a dull sentence.* Calling baseball America's belly-button—

*Bill Lee, nicknamed "spaceman," pitched for the Boston Red Sox from 1969 through 1978 and for the Montreal Expos from 1979 until his retirement in 1982. The left-handed pitcher was a source of many startling and original quotes over the years. (The one used as the epigraph of this chapter appeared in the *Los Angeles Times* on Feb. 3, 1977.) An extremely effective pitcher, with a lifetime record of 119–90, that primal remnant of everyone's first medium of nourishment and entry into the world—is exactly right, just as reverential descriptions of the game as a metaphor for and evidence of American exceptionalism and goodness are exactly wrong (unless, for a moment, one succumbs to national pride after being congratulated on the game in a far-off land). Baseball matters because it provides genuine nourishment rather than junk food (a good hot dog is *not* junk food). I have concentrated on baseball's vulnerabilities in today's culture precisely because we cannot afford to lose a game that demands our attention to provide its nourishment. Many have argued that baseball has outlived its time, as the Ringling Brothers and Barnum & Bailey Circus had when it gave its final performance in 2017 after years of declining ticket sales. This analogy is misplaced. The circus folded for a specific cultural reason: there has been a sea change during the past two decades in public attitudes about the confinement and exhibition of animals for entertainment. For increasing numbers of parents in their thirties and forties, taking children to see performing elephants and tigers ran counter to important ethical values.

Baseball, as we have seen, is also vulnerable to outside cul-

---

Lee had one bad moment on the mound that will be remembered forever in Boston. In the seventh game of the 1975 World Series, with Boston up 3–0 in the sixth inning, he throw an eephus pitch to Cincinnati slugger Tony Pérez, who hit a two-run homer to begin the Reds' comeback. An eephus pitch is an extremely slow pitch, almost a lob, and if used judiciously, it usually fools hitters completely. Pérez, the future Hall of Famer, was not fooled.

tural changes, but the changes have little to do with ethics and everything to do with technology and the altered nature of childhood in a culture gorging on entertainment. But I do not think that baseball will go the way of the circus, because the game has played a role in American history that goes far beyond amusement or entertainment.

The role of the Civil War in spreading baseball across the nation, far beyond the northeastern states where the game began, is the first example of baseball's complicated relationship with America's iconic image of itself. Union soldiers from the Middle West, many of whom had never been exposed to baseball before serving in the army, learned the game from their contact, during the prolonged waiting times in encampments between battles, with soldiers from the Northeast who already played and understood the prematurely named national pastime. Some Union officers actually sent reports to their superiors recommending that baseball be promoted in encampments in order to keep the minds of soldiers off the war. Baseball equipment was a problem. The standard "ball" was a walnut wrapped with yarn until a piece of horsehide would fit around it tightly. Branches of oak trees were cut down and carved into bats. Special baseball gloves did not yet exist.[1] After the war, surviving Union soldiers brought baseball back to their communities and taught it to their children, laying the basis for the national game as an ordinary person's recreation as well as a professional sport. In the decade after the Civil War, baseball in the North spread from "the region of the Manhattanese" to the northern plains states, where the summer playing season was short and the first snowflakes might appear as early as September.

The Civil War also spread the game to the South, but southerners learned how to play in prison camps—not only if they were imprisoned in the North, but from Union soldiers imprisoned within the Confederacy. Our image of Civil War prisons (insofar as it survives) is formed mainly by the most notorious institutions, such as Andersonville in Georgia and Elmira in New York. Treatment of prisoners in camps became more brutal after 1863, when all prisoner exchanges were suspended by the Union because the Confederate Army treated captured black soldiers not as prisoners of war but as the property of their former masters—even if the master was unknown or nonexistent. After President Lincoln signed the Emancipation Proclamation on January 1, 1863, the Union Army stepped up recruitment of black soldiers. From the Confederacy's viewpoint, all black soldiers were former slaves—whether or not they had actually lived in the South or been slaves under pre–Civil War laws. A black soldier captured by the Confederate Army had almost no chance of coming home alive. In the days when exchanges were still possible, however, baseball games were played in both northern and southern prison camps.

One of the earliest known visual depictions of such prison games—indeed, of baseball itself—belongs to the collection of the Smithsonian Institution's National Museum of American History. It is a lithograph by the artist Otto Botticher (sometimes spelled Boetticher), who was himself a prisoner of war. Botticher, a Prussian immigrant and a successful portrait painter in New York before the war, was captured near Manassas, Virginia. In North Carolina's Salisbury Confederate Prison, he produced a watercolor of an 1862 ballgame, and the watercolor served as the basis for the lithograph after Botticher was released in a prisoner exchange. The Salisbury facility was specifically designed to hold Union officers waiting to be exchanged for Confederate officers, and because the prisoners were considered to be officers and gentlemen, they enjoyed a great many privileges that would disappear after 1863. Soldiers documented their daily pastimes in diaries. "Prisoners from the first half of 1862 noted that baseball games were played nearly every day, weather permitting," notes Debbie Schaefer-Jacobs, a curator at the National Museum of American History. "For the first couple of years, prisoners were also permitted to whittle, read, write letters, attend lectures, perform 'theatrics,' play cards such as poker, and go fishing."[2] The lithograph of Union prisoners playing ball depicts an audience that included townspeople as well as guards. The picture definitely presents a pro-southern view of the treatment of captives in Confederate prisons and was promoted that way in Europe. However, the lithograph was also marketed in northern American states and, according to Schaefer-Jacobs, was popular there for "the images of Union officers and of course for the depiction of a baseball game in progress."[3] With the baseball diamond as its focal point, the lithograph has a slightly pastoral as well as propagandistic quality; were it not for two guards holding guns, it could be assumed that this ballgame was taking place on some sort of village green. This impression is reinforced not only by the lithograph's focus on the ballgame but by the presence of small cottages, a meatpacking plant, a blacksmith shop, and even a small hospital in what was, in fact, a prison compound. Needless to say, there are no black people—soldiers or civilians—in this picture.

It is one of the ironies of baseball history that the game truly became America's "national pastime" only after a war in which more than 620,000 soldiers died. The unfinished business of that war—America's resistance to racial equality in the North and South—meant that baseball would develop, on both a semi-professional and a professional basis—as a largely segregated national pastime. This development was not inevitable—not, at least, until the end of Reconstruction and the rise of Jim Crow. There were a few nineteenth-century blacks—their names unknown to almost everyone today except scholars of baseball—who played for professional teams in the first two decades after the Civil War. Moses Fleetwood "Fleet" Walker caught for the Toledo Blue Stockings of the then–major league American Association in the early 1880s, and his brother Welday also played a few games in the outfield for the team. Fleet Walker attracted the racial animus—actually, "hatred" is the correct word—of Adrian "Cap" Anson, an enormously influential figure in the history of baseball who played twenty-seven seasons at first base, mainly for the Chicago White Stockings (who eventually became the Cubs, not the White Sox). Born in Marshalltown, Iowa, Anson became the first player to reach 3,000 hits—and he was also an ardent segregationist. Anson, who was inducted into the Hall of Fame in 1939, refused to play against a team with a black man on the field. In 1884, according to various scholars, the Chicago team asked for assurances that Fleet Walker would not be on the field at an exhibition game with Toledo.

This evolved into the infamous "gentlemen's agreement" that prevented blacks from playing in the major leagues until 1947. Some gentlemen. In the official exhibition on Anson in Coopers-town, former Hall of Fame historian Lee Allen described Anson thus: "Sturdy, blunt, and honest . . . the captain who was always kicking at decisions, the symbol of all that was strong and good in baseball."[4] This is indeed a description worthy of inclusion in the Baseball Hall of Shame. Anson wasn't the only villain in the so-called gentlemen's agreement. Many of Walker's own team-mates shunned him. According to one baseball historian, Toledo pitcher Tony Mullane would "intentionally throw the ball in the dirt, trying to injure his own battery mate."[5]

In the decades after the institutionalization of segregation in professional baseball, blacks could and did watch white baseball—usually from separate blocs of seats—and whites could and did watch black baseball. But the playing field itself never offered the possibility of equality, any more than a great many trains, hotels, and restaurants did. Whatever patriotic associations were fostered by and embedded in baseball, turning a blind eye to segregation was part of the deal. In his essay "My Baseball Years," Philip Roth writes about his own feelings of patriotism when he attended minor league games in Newark during the Second World War.

> It would have seemed to me an emotional thrill forsaken if, before the Newark Bears took on the hated enemy from across the marshes, the Jersey City Giants, we hadn't first to rise to our feet

(my father, my brother, and I—along with our inimical country-
men, the city's Germans, Irish, Poles, and, out in the Africa of the
bleachers, Newark's Negroes) to celebrate the America that had
given to this unharmonious mob a game so grand and beautiful.[6]

The Africa of the bleachers. Much has been written about the
importance of baseball in the Americanization of immigrants
and their children from the early 1900s through the Second
World War. Not least among the factors contributing to Americanization was the fact that by the time Roth was a young fan,
the sons of first-generation immigrants had established themselves as stars of the game. Among the most prominent were
Lou Gehrig, whose background as the son of German immigrants helped make an enthusiastic fan out of my grandmother;
Hank Greenberg, born on the Lower East Side to Romanian
Jewish immigrants; and Joe DiMaggio, the eighth of nine children born to Sicilian immigrant parents. But black Americans,
whose families had been in the United States for hundreds of
years, were relegated not only to the Africa of the bleachers in
professional parks but to the Africa of the Negro Leagues. It
is not an exaggeration to say that the desegregation of baseball
in 1947 was as much a part of the unfinished business of the
Civil War as the desegregation of the military was in 1948. But
it had taken another war and another eighty-plus years to move
both baseball and the military toward some semblance of justice
—another demonstration of why baseball's identification with
American values matters and why those values continue to demand close scrutiny. Yet who could have imagined in 1941 that
an unknown Jack Roosevelt Robinson, who would be drafted,

be assigned to a segregated unit (there were no others, of course), and narrowly survive an attempt to court-martial him for refusing to move to the back of an army bus, would break the color barrier in baseball only two years after the war's end. Baseball desegregated, with difficulty and dissension, not because it was the right thing to do (although some exceptional men, like Bill Veeck and Branch Rickey, recognized that it was) but because M.L.B. needed the talent of great black players. Desegregation was based on baseball's pragmatic needs, not idealism. But that is not an indictment of the game. One can only wish that the nation's finest educational institutions and most successful businesses had come to the same realization as early as 1947.

At the beginning of the 2017 season, baseball fans were reminded that their country's racial divide is still a part of being taken out to the ballgame. Calvin Hennick, a white fan of the Boston Red Sox, had taken his biracial son, Nile, to see a game at Fenway Park as an early sixth birthday present. He was attending the game not only with his son but with his African-American father-in-law. As it happened, this game took place May 3—one night after Adam Jones, an African-American center fielder for the Baltimore Orioles, had been the target of a racial slur by a Boston fan. At the game attended by Hennick's family, the national anthem was sung by a Kenyan woman. Then, according to the *Boston Globe,* a middle-aged white man, wearing a Red Sox cap and T-shirt, leaned over Hennick and used a racial epithet to characterize the Kenyan woman's rendition of "The Star-Spangled Banner." Hennick notified Red Sox security, and the fan was ejected from the park and barred for life. Before calling security,

Hennick had actually asked the man to repeat his words. He thought he might have misheard and "wanted to be 100 percent sure I heard him right."[7]

After the two incidents in Fenway, M.L.B. announced that it was reviewing its security procedure in all ballparks to determine how racial and ethnic slurs were being handled. This story was especially stinging to me because I remember, so clearly, how shocked I was to hear Robinson called a "nigger" at Wrigley Field in the early 1950s. Back then, however, no one was ejected at Wrigley for spewing forth the same racist words that fans shouted at Fenway in 2017. It is tragic that young Nile Hennick, excited about his forthcoming birthday and seeing his Red Sox, could not be protected from hearing the same filth that I heard in Chicago more than sixty years ago. The difference is that this young boy also saw a man thrown out of the ballpark for using racist language. Furthermore, I can imagine what the adult Cubs fans in the early 1950s would have had to say to a white man attending a ballgame with his biracial child and black father-in-law. A baseball park in any era is, after all, only one venue for the display of the best and the worst of American values. For racial slurs to disappear from ballparks altogether, Americans would have to construct the postracial society that is still so far beyond us.

In no historical period was baseball's connection with American identity more complicated than during the Second World War. More than five hundred major league players served in the military. They included many stars of the game—DiMaggio,

Greenberg, Ralph Kiner, Ted Williams, Stan Musial, and Bob Feller, to name only a few. All returned home, resumed their careers, and eventually wound up in the Hall of Fame, but devotees of statistics still love to figure out how much better the lifetime records would have been had the athletes not lost several prime playing years to war. Five weeks after Pearl Harbor, Judge Kenesaw Mountain Landis, then the commissioner of baseball, wrote President Franklin D. Roosevelt and asked whether baseball should continue during the war. The following day, in what came to be known as the "green light letter," Roosevelt wrote Landis, "I honestly feel that it would be best for the country to keep baseball going." He noted that Americans would be working longer hours than before the war and argued, "That means they ought to have the chance for recreation and for taking their minds off their work more than ever before."[8] The quality of ball played in the United States undoubtedly suffered during the war, since players who were declared unfit for combat by military doctors tended to be older than the stars who were in the prime of their careers. There certainly would have been serious questions about draft evasion had the greatest stars of the game, obviously in first-rate physical condition, somehow been declared unfit to serve. In an article prepared for a symposium on baseball and culture at the Hall of Fame, two scholars note that in spite of the military service of many top players, there was some criticism from within the Roosevelt administration itself. James Byrnes, director of war mobilization and reconstruction, wondered how players could be declared physically unfit for service if they were still physically fit to play baseball. M.L.B. gave the not entirely convincing answer that players had training room support not available in the military, and "after all, they were found to be 4-F by army and navy doctors, not baseball's doctors."[9]

There is little doubt that most Americans approved of the decision to continue baseball during the war, and baseball was played by the troops wherever fields could be carved out adjacent to military encampments. There is even an iconic photograph—reminiscent of the Civil War prison lithograph—showing marines in the Solomon Islands studying their position on the map while also poring over baseball scores. The photo was published in the Marine Corps' *Guadalcanal Gazette*.[10] Roosevelt was right. I like to think of these young men, not knowing whether they would ever return from what, at that time, seemed like an uphill battle against Japan, feeling a link to home that had nothing to do with bombs, shells, shrapnel, and death. I like to imagine those scared kids hoping that they might one day see or play a game in which no one had to die.

Japan as an enemy, however, posed something of a problem for the baseball establishment, which included the sporting press. The nation that attacked the United States at Pearl Harbor had embraced baseball since the 1870s. The game was imported by the American missionary Horace Wilson, who taught at an institution of higher education that is now Tokyo University. Baseball became so popular, and so respected, in Japan that the game received a Japanese name—*yakyu*. All other sports that trace their origins to foreign countries—such as football, soccer, tennis, basketball, and golf—are known only by their foreign names in Japan.

In 1934, a team of American all-stars, headed by Babe Ruth, toured Japan to enormous popular acclaim and competed with the Nippon all-stars. Jimmie Foxx, the second American player to hit more than 500 home runs (after Ruth), was also on the tour, and he captured the camaraderie and excitement in eight-millimeter, black-and-white film, now digitized and stored in the Hall of Fame. Japan—the only nation in Asia or Europe to fall in love with the American national pastime, was now our mortal enemy. What did this mean about the sanctified American values supposedly embodied by baseball? As one historian of the military and baseball puts it, "If baseball embodied those values that made America great, such as fair play, hustle, and teamwork, did Japan's love of the game mean that the Japanese exhibited these qualities as well?"[11]

Just eleven days after Pearl Harbor, J. G. Taylor Spink, editor of the *Sporting News,* addressed the issue in an editorial. Baseball, he explained (in a burst of venom that did not do justice to Horace Wilson or his nineteenth-century Japanese students) was not a recent phenomenon in Japan.

> It dates back some 70 years, not so long after our American Civil War. It was introduced by American missionaries, who wanted to wean their boy pupils away from such native sports as the stupid Japanese wrestling, fencing with crude broadswords, and jiu-jitsu. Having a natural catlike agility, the Japanese took naturally to the diamond pastime. They became first-class fielders and made some, progress in pitching, but because of their smallness of stature, they remained feeble hitters. In their games with visiting American teams, it was always a sore spot with this cocky race that their batsmen were so outclasssed by the stronger, more powerful Amer-

ican sluggers. For, despite the brusqueness and braggadocio of the militarists, Japanese cockiness hid a natural inferiority complex.

Spink concluded that Japan was never truly "converted" to baseball, despite its enormous popularity before the war. "They may have acquired a little skill at the game," he told his readers, "but the soul of our National Game never touched them. No nation which has had as intimate contact with baseball as the Japanese, could have committed the vicious, infamous deed of the early morning of December 7, 1941, if the spirit of the game had ever penetrated their yellow hides."[12]

Take that, you slant-eyes! Yes, the Japanese, with their feline agility, might have learned how to turn a nifty double play, but they could never really comprehend or partake of the goodness and purity of America's game. Spink's rationale certainly did embody the American values that led to the imprisonment of Japanese Americans in concentration camps during the war. This is not the belly-button of our society but an anatomical opening located somewhat lower in our body politic. It is to be hoped that when Ichiro Suzuki becomes the first Japanese-born and Japanese-bred player elevated to the baseball Hall of Fame, a copy of this editorial will be prominently displayed in the exhibit dedicated to him. I have no doubt that the Hall of Fame will meet its historical responsibility in this regard. During the past forty years, the Hall in Cooperstown has transformed itself from a curio institution that pretty much ignored baseball's sins into a serious historical museum and scholarly research center. Many scholars trace the beginning of that transformation to

1971, when Satchel Paige became the first veteran of the Negro Leagues inducted into the Hall. Public protest had forced the Hall to abandon its insulting original plan to hang Paige's plaque in a separate section from the other members of the Hall and to place his image where it belonged—with the other baseball immortals. "This notion of Jim Crow in Baseball's Heaven is appalling," wrote Jim Murray, a columnist for the *Los Angeles Times,* in 1971. "What is this—1840? Either let him in the front of the Hall—or move the damn thing to Mississippi."[13] Today, a life-size bronze statue of Paige in his characteristic windup stands on the south lawn of the Hall.

If there were any doubt that baseball still occupies a special place in America's iconic image of its best self, and a conflicted place whenever America's worst impulses bare their teeth, it should have been erased by the mixture of horror and sanctimony expressed in the aftermath of the shooting of four people on June 14, 2017, at a Republican practice for the annual congressional baseball game. The majority whip of the House of Representatives, Steve Scalise; two congressional staff aides; and a Capitol police officer were wounded during a practice session in Alexandria, Virginia, just across the Potomac River from the nation's capital. The shooter, killed by a Capitol policeman who was part of the detail guarding Scalise, was James T. Hodgkinson, a sixty-six-year-old from Belleville, Illinois, who turned out to be a familiar figure in the annals of American killings—an unstable man with a history of domestic violence, a powerful rifle (which he was perfectly free to buy despite his record), and a political grievance. A volunteer in Bernie Sanders's primary campaign against Hillary Clinton, he had expressed strong animus toward Donald Trump and had come to Washington with what looked like a hit list of Republican members of the House and Senate.

In short, Hodgkinson was the usual made-in-America, gun-toting crazy, this time on the left side of the political spectrum. Hodgkinson got lucky; the practice ball field was one of the few largely unguarded places where a group of congressional representatives might go. Had Scalise not been a member of the House leadership, and therefore guarded by a police detail, the body count would have been much higher.

This attack had no more to do with baseball than the terrorist mass murder at an Orlando nightclub a year and two days earlier in 2016 had to do with nightclubs per se. Yet much of the commentary for the first twenty-four hours after the shootings focused on baseball itself. A column in the *New York Times* by Steve Israel, a former New York Democratic congressman, was headlined "An Attack on Congress and Baseball." The publicity was so intense that the killings of three workers at a United Parcel Service facility in San Francisco, by another deranged gunman who killed himself, were all but ignored. Nor were there any headlines suggesting that the San Francisco murders had been "an attack on package delivery services."

Representative Roger Williams, a Republican from Texas, declared, in an interview with CNN, "America doesn't give out; America doesn't give in and we must play this baseball game. If we don't play this baseball game and we go home, then they win. . . . This is America, the greatest country in the world. If you punch us, we punch back. And we're going to play baseball to-morrow."[14] The use of pronouns in this interview deserves special attention. "If we don't play this baseball game, then *they* win." "If *you* punch us, we punch back." To whom do *they* and *you* refer? It sounds almost as if Williams thought the shooter was a non-American terrorist who hated baseball. The undertone here is that that shooting men in the process of playing baseball was a form of sacrilege as well as a crime. More than twenty-five thousand people who bought tickets for the game seemed to agree; the amount of money raised for charity was more than a million dollars—more than twice the amount raised the previous year. The enthusiasm even spilled over to another, less publicized annual event, a charity softball game between female members of Congress and members of the Capitol Hill press corps. The congressional game was played at the Washington Nationals' stadium, but the women's softball game took place on Capitol Hill, on a scruffy artificial turf football field that had been appropriated and repurposed for the night. In 2017, the bleachers were jammed as the correspondents, named the Bad News Babes, beat the lawmakers 2–1. A female Capitol police officer injured in the shootings threw out the first pitch.

Why does this episode bother me so much? Surely there is nothing wrong with thousands of extra people forking over money for charity or with women getting a small, unaccustomed piece of the action. The problem here is that baseball, our beautiful game of largely native origins, was being used as a metaphor for a kind of mindless "punch-me-I'll-punch-you-harder" ethos. This martial attitude is even more ridiculous because the enemy of America and baseball who committed the crime was indisputably One of Us.

There is no question that baseball, even though it is no longer the most popular American sport, still lends itself to a unique conflation of the game itself with American virtue. The response to the shootings in Washington, despite being attached to a less cosmic event, inevitably reminded me, as a New Yorker, of the role baseball played in my city after the terrorist attacks of September 11, 2001. The first thing I did on September 13, when the city was open for business again, was buy tickets for a game scheduled for September 21 between the Mets and the Atlanta Braves. It wasn't an important game, but I had planned to see it anyway because the regular baseball season was almost over. I was certain that this game would be played and that New Yorkers would turn out in droves—not to "punch back" at the terrorists but to demonstrate that we were going to continue with our normal lives. The game was a sellout—at a time when many New Yorkers were still too fearful to take the subway. And I cannot deny that I felt something, while singing "Take Me Out to the Ball Game" as a citizen in the company of my fellow citizens, that I could never have felt at a theatrical performance or, for that matter, a football game. The emotions baseball is capable of evoking are part of its special currency, but it is a currency that can easily be devalued if used in an exclusionary, aggressive fashion.

There was nothing unduly bombastic about President George W. Bush's appearance in Yankee Stadium on October 30, 2001, to throw out the first pitch of the third game of the World Series between the Yankees and the Arizona Diamondbacks. Bush, as is well known, has deep and authentic ties to baseball as a former owner of the Texas Rangers. Furthermore, his speech to rescue workers, delivered through a bullhorn amid the ruins of Ground Zero, had endeared him to the many New Yorkers who voted against him. It might have been something of an insult had he *not* shown up in the Bronx to throw the first pitch.

But a video of Bush's two appearances, shown at the Republican National Convention in 2004, is another matter altogether.* Linking Bush's "bullhorn moment" with his moment on the mound, the video was introduced by then-Senator Fred Thompson of Tennessee (who chose not to run for reelection in order to play a tough district attorney on NBC's long-running *Law and Order* series). In his narration, Thompson said of Bush, "He was wearing a heavy secret service bulletproof vest, and he could hardly move his arms. But he knew. So George Bush took the mound. What he did that night—the man in the arena—he helped us come back. That's the story of this presidency. With the heart of a president, he told us, 'You keep pitching. No matter what, you keep pitching. No matter what, you go to the mound, you find the plate, and you throw. And you become who you are.'" Thompson then asked, in grave tones reminiscent of 1950s television shows exalting the FBI, "What do a bullhorn and a baseball have in common? What truths can they tell? Which is

---

*I am indebted to Michael L. Butterworth, author of *Baseball and Rhetorics of Purity,* for reminding me about the video, which I slept through on the night it was broadcast at the 2004 convention.

another way of saying, What did George W. Bush do? What did he become? And how did that help us?"[15] In *Rhetorics of Purity*, Michael Butterworth deconstructs this mystifying analogy between throwing a pitch and defending one's country. "On the one hand," he writes, "baseball appears as a metaphor in the conventional sense—that is, the game serves as a model of national character and unity in a time of crisis. . . . Yet, on the other hand, the convention video also depends on a . . . logic that hails baseball as a means for shaping attitudes and behaviors. In other words, Bush did not throw the first pitch at the World Series merely to exploit baseball as a clever persuasive strategy. Instead, *the video tells us that the very act of throwing from the Yankee Stadium mound that evening transformed the man himself*."[16]

What do a bullhorn and a baseball have in common? Absolutely nothing.

Baseball's relationship to American values—however one defines them—has never been "pure" and has always been as complicated as the physical and mental game unfolding on the field. The capacity of baseball to reinvent itself at certain crucial points in American history—even when the reinvention has proceeded too slowly—is the essence of the game's importance as the belly-button of our society. When one reads Spink's wartime denunciation of "feline" Japanese as beings too lowly to enter into the soul of baseball, the international sport we take for granted today—in terms of foreign-born players on American teams and the popularity of the game throughout much of Asia and Latin America —seems almost miraculous. At the same time, baseball has never gotten too far ahead of other American institutions in reinventions of a cultural nature. Robinson and his black baseball contemporaries differed only in their athletic skills from the tens of thousands of black Americans who had served their country in wartime and who returned home with the strong sense that America owed them more opportunity than they had ever received in the past (or in segregated military units).

What baseball has never had to do in nearly a century, since the transition from the dead ball to the lively ball era, is reinvent the way the game is actually played in order to attract a new generation of fans. Much as I dislike the designated hitter, I do not consider it a major reinvention. Baseball is played in essentially the same way as it was when my grandfather watched it as a teenager a century ago and when he passed it on to me as a child in the 1950s. That seamless transition is no longer occurring, as I have emphasized throughout this book—and that is why baseball, at all levels, must make more of an effort than it has been making to attract new younger fans of all ethnic and racial groups and to bring more of its traditional fan base—especially African Americans—back to the ballpark, as well as to the interior stadium.

In the past, new technology (even if many owners failed to understand this at the time) was always baseball's friend. Every change was perfectly suited to the expansion of the long game in the American imagination. After the Civil War, the greater reach of railroads was a perfect enabler for the nationwide extension of the baseball knowledge that soldiers had acquired in encampments and prisons, in both the North and the South. The first transcontinental railroad—its construction having begun in 1863, during one of the darkest periods of the war—was completed in 1869, thereby ensuring that baseball (among other enterprises) would reach the American West. In the interval between the First and Second World Wars, radio would make fans out of people who had never seen a professional game at the minor or major league level. The same would be true of television in the 1950s, despite the laments of those who, by then, were insisting that listening to radio was the only right way to experience a game outside the ballpark.

The online world is different, in that its devices are designed not to focus anyone's attention on a long game, in either the literal or metaphoric senses, but to enable split focus. While it would be foolish for baseball not to make use of every available form of technology to reach young fans, it would be even more foolish for stewards of the game to deform the essence of their unique product—to twist the belly-button further, as Bill Lee might put it, instead of to straighten it out. Baseball should not run away from its strongest selling points—the tension of un-timed confrontations between hitter and pitcher; the intricacy of a team sport in which one never loses sight of individuals; the contrast between the solitude of the interior stadium and friendships born out of (and borne along by) endless talk about the game, and, above all, a sense of history that can be felt even before its particulars are known.

Finally, the future of baseball depends not only on its institutions but on individual adult fans making an effort to show the young why we love the game and why they might love it too if they surrendered themselves, as an experiment, to time uninterrupted by clocks and clicks. Such experiments can work—if the grown-ups invest their hearts and their own time in teaching. A few years ago, I used Lawrence Ritter's 1966 classic *The Glory of Their Times: The Story of the Early Days of Baseball Told by the Men Who Played It* in a volunteer tutoring program for children considered smart but unmotivated. My eleven-year-old-student became enthralled by the voices of men from a time he had initially dismissed as "boring." His general interest in both history and baseball increased dramatically; he would phone me to ask what a crackerjack or an agnostic or an atheist was (all terms used by players born in the nineteenth century). My young student picked up the words "agnostic" and "atheist" from Ritter's interview with Sam Crawford, known as "Wahoo Sam," who played from 1899 to 1917 and was the dominant power hitter of the dead-ball era. Wahoo Sam was a fan of Robert Green Ingersoll, who was known as the "Great Agnostic" in the last quarter of the nineteenth century. He certainly might have heard Ingersoll's speeches in the early 1890s, and he agreed with the Great Agnostic's favorite admonition, "Let the dead past bury its dead." Although Crawford did go on to reference George Santayana's well-known line about those who cannot remember the past being condemned to repeat it. "So maybe there are two sides to this matter," Crawford told Ritter.[17]

I was initially surprised that my young student perused these interviews so closely, and followed digressions like Wahoo Sam's musings on just about everything, because I had been told that this boy was an extremely poor reader. He especially loved the biblical quote used by Ritter as an epigraph: "All these were honoured in their generations, and were the glory of their times."

This is why baseball matters and why it matters even more today than it did in the past. The game stands up and out in the lowest-common-denominator American culture of distraction, disruption, and interruption. For me, this distinction makes baseball the most intellectual stimulating, emotionally satisfying, and downright glorious pastime ever devised. I see it as the duty—yes, a genuine patriotic duty in the best sense—of all of us who love the game to do everything we can to see that baseball continues to matter. One kid at a time, one adult at a time.

afterword: susan's suggestions to owners,
players, and anyone else who cares

1. Hire a tech-savvy kid to design a software program aimed at
helping elementary school children learn math through learning baseball. Better yet, hold a nationwide competition (something like the
National Spelling Bee) with a prize for the student who comes up
with the best teaching tool. Offer the prize-winning software program
free to public schools. I owe this idea to my late uncle, Oswald Jacoby,
a newspaper columnist and a bridge and backgammon champion from
the 1930s until his death in 1984. He wanted to use both poker and
bridge to teach math in the 1960s—when he felt children's math skills
were declining—but no schools took him up on it. Poker may have
been the sticking point. Sadly, my uncle died before the era of personal computers, for which he would certainly have crafted a program
himself.

2. Offer free seats for every afternoon game to every child under fifteen who comes to the ballpark with an adult. The early teens, according to every study, are the age when the young—even if they played
baseball in elementary school—begin to lose interest. Accompaniment
by an adult is important to encourage families to attend. Advertise
these games unceasingly.

3. Inundate women's organizations with information about the rel-

ative safety of baseball as a sport for children. Parents of both sexes are increasingly concerned about youthful concussions, and this is a particularly strong selling point for mothers. Make a special point of reaching out to African-American women's organizations, given baseball's need to draw more black fans as well as young fans. The point is not only to get more mothers to come to ballgames with their children but to persuade mothers to encourage their children to play baseball.

4. Make fluency in English a mandatory aspect of player development in the minor leagues. This means you, Major League Baseball, and you, the Major League Baseball Players Association. You know that only 10 percent of minor league players ever get to play in the majors. This is an issue that primarily affects Hispanic players today, since Asian players are usually stars in their own countries before they come to play in the United States. I know, I know, M.L.B. talks about its English instruction in Dominican academies, but few of the graduates speak English well even when they reach the major leagues after spending time in the minor leagues in the United States. Being able to talk to the press is part of the job. For the 90 percent of minor leaguers who do not make it to the majors, having spent years without learning English means they are unfit for any other decently paid job in the United States. There are some first-generation Hispanic Americans with the same problem. If Dominican and Hispanic-American players do get to the majors, inability to express themselves in English will deprive them of some of the recognition they deserve. And if they don't—well, you have taken their young years and left them with no nonbaseball education. Improving English instruction and treating it as a part of baseball training will help baseball develop its young stars, and—oh, yes—it's the right thing to do.

5. Day games should be the rule, not the exception, on weekends—during the regular season and the postseason. (This is my least original suggestion, and I know it's not going to happen because it isn't what sponsors want. But it certainly would expand the school-age audience for baseball.)

6. Make special outreach efforts to girls in your Play Ball program for young children. I know the program is open to everyone, but in every picture I see of these groups, nearly everyone is a boy. Are girls not interested, or do they feel unwelcome? Just asking.

7. When you take a kid to a ballgame, give her an interesting baseball book afterward. There are so many wonderful books about baseball that it should be possible to find the right one for every child. Try both the sublime (for example, Lawrence Ritter's *The Glory of Their Times*) and the ridiculous (like *The Baseball Hall of Shame,* by Bruce Nash and Allen Zullo).

8. Think twice about investments in commercial fantasy baseball operations that are really a way of making money from sports gambling. You know, owners. You know, players. Anytime baseball has become involved with gambling, however indirectly, it doesn't turn out well. I know that fantasy baseball games can't be "fixed" in the way that a real game can be fixed by the deliberate malfeasance of star players. But trying to hook younger fans by investing in entities that may, in turn, hook them on a potential vice as old as recorded history is, well, unworthy of the national pastime. "Statsy" fans who aren't compulsive gamblers and who want to play fantasy sports will do so anyway.

9. Tony Clark, the head of the players' union, has talked frequently about the need for baseball to promote its stars in order to attract young fans. We all know about the epidemic of opioid addiction in this country. How about sending some of your young stars to schools, youth groups, and events like the Little League World Series, to talk about the dangers of opioid use? You think kids wouldn't take the word of Aaron Judge or Jacob deGrom over lectures from their parents or the high school nurse? Conspicuous community service is one of the best ways to showcase players—and it might even save some lives.

10. Oh, please, revisit, and revisit again, plans to attract more young baseball fans by instituting changes that will make the game less like . . . well, baseball. Remember the mistake that the Coca-Cola company made back in the 1980s when it tried to attract Pepsi drinkers by pro-

ducing the sickly sweet abomination called New Coke. No business ever reinvented itself by abandoning its unique selling propositions, regardless of how tempting that bogus solution always is to short-term thinkers. Baseball's unique selling propositions are timelessness, logic, and history. Successful marketers, while they're always adding on to the basic appeal of their products, are, above all, people who can present their traditional product in a more interesting way. How about a marketing campaign based on an idea like "Baseball: The Grownup Game for Kids"? Market the real thing.

The flag (W) indicates a source available only on the Web.

INTRODUCTION

Epigraph. Versions of this quote have also been attributed to a number of players and managers, including Yogi Berra. It seems safe to stick with the common attribution to Casey Stengel, given that he seems to have said practically everything there is to say about the game.

1. Written with John Hough, Jr., the book was published by Harcourt Brace Jovanovich.

ONE: THE GOOD AND BAD OLD DAYS

1. See Maury Brown, "Baseball Is Dying: TV Ratings for 2016 World Series Through the Roof," Nov. 3, 2016, www.forbes.com (W); A. J. Perez, "World Series TV Ratings: Epic Game 7 Was Off the Charts," *USA Today,* Nov. 3, 2016.

2. See Tyler Kepner, "All Power to the State of the Sport, for Better or Worse," *New York Times,* July 12, 2017.

3. Jay Kaspian Kang, "Diamonds and Rust," *New York Times Magazine,* April 2, 2017.

4. "President Herbert Hoover Baseball-Related Quotations," www.baseball-almanac.com (W).

5. "Reserve Clause," BR Bullpen, www.baseball-reference.com (W).

6. In Roger Angell, "The Long Green," *Late Innings* (New York, 1982), p. 30.

7. George W. Mitchell, *Report to the Commissioner of Baseball of an Independent Investigation into the Illegal Use of Steroids and Other Performance Enhancing Substances by Players in Major League Baseball,* Dec. 31, 2007, p. 1.

8. Pete Rose/A. Bartlett Giamatti Agreement, Aug. 24, 1989, http://www.baseball-almanac.com (W).

9. Jacques Barzun, *God's Country and Mine* (Boston, 1954), p. 159.

10. Ibid., pp. 162–63.

11. Ibid., p. 160.

12. In Douglas McDaniel, "Jacques Barzun, 'Baseball's Best Cultural Critic,' Turns His Back on Game," www.bleacherreport.com (W).

13. Cited in Jules Tygiel, *Past Time: Baseball as History* (New York, 2000), p. 6.

14. Maury Brown, "M.L.B. Sponsorships in 2016 Will Reap $360–$400 Million to Already Robust Bottom Line," *Forbes,* Oct. 25, 2016.

15. See Scott Lindholm, "Major League Attendance Trends Past, Present, and Future," Feb. 10, 2014, SB Nation—A Saber-Slanted Baseball Community, www.beyondtheboxscore.com (W).

16. Cited in Tygiel, *Past Time,* p. 72.

17. Interview with the author.

18. Quoted in Bill Pennington, "They Can Hit a Ball 400 Feet. But Play Catch? That's Tricky," *New York Times,* April 2, 2017.

19. David G. Ogden, "The Demise of African-American Participa-

tion in Baseball: A Cultural Backlash from the Negro Leagues," Nov. 1, 2005 (W).

20. Alan Klein, *Dominican Baseball: New Pride, Old Prejudice* (Philadelphia, 2014), p. 32.

21. In Susan Jacoby, "Baseball and Its Aging Fans," *Wall Street Journal,* Aug. 20–21, 2016.

TWO: PATIENCE

1. See Phil Vettel, "The Cubs Get Lights at Wrigley Field," *Chicago Tribune,* © 2017, www.chicagotribune.com (W).

2. Interview with the author.

3. David Kagan, "The Physics of Wind at the Remodeled Wrigley Field," *Hardball Times,* Sept. 16, 2015, www.hardballtimes.com (W).

4. Billy Witz, "On Windy Day at Wrigley, Yankees Beat Cubs on Gardner's Homer," *New York Times,* May 6, 2017.

5. Mike Vaccaro, "Syndergaard Is Damning Proof of Mets' Senseless Injury Charade," *New York Post,* April 30, 2017.

6. Roger Angell, "Distance," in *Late Innings* (New York, 1982), pp. 260–92.

7. See William F. McNeil, *The Evolution of Pitching in Major League Baseball* (Jefferson, N.C., 2006).

8. See Baseball Hall of Fame profile, www.baseballhall.org.

9. In Joe Frisaro and Roger Rubin, "5-Run 7th Caps Rally as Mets Down Marlins," Major League Baseball, May 6, 2017 (W). This story was not subject to the approval of M.L.B., the Mets, or the Marlins.

10. Greg Stoll, Win Expectancy Finder, www.gregstoll.com (W).

11. Ibid.

12. Carey K. Morewedge, "It Was a Most Unusual Time: How Memory Bias Engenders Nostalgic Preference," *Journal of Behavioral Decision Making,* October 2013.

13. In Roger Angell, "Not So, Boston," *Season Ticket* (Boston, 1988), p. 311.

14. Ibid., p. 341.

15. Larry Tye, *Satchel: The Life and Times of an American Legend* (New York, 2010), p. ix.

16. Satchel Paige's "Six Rules for a Long Life," *Collier's,* June 13, 1953.

17. Jay Caspian Kang, "Where Did the Great Hollywood Baseball Movie Go?" *New York Times Magazine,* May 23, 2017.

18. Jules Tygiel, *Past Time: Baseball as History* (New York, 2000), p. 202.

19. Ibid.

THREE: WHO GOES OUT TO THE BALLGAME AND WHO DOESN'T?

1. Nielsen Sports, analysis prepared for the author in July 2016.

2. Nielsen Sports, analysis prepared for the author in May 2017.

3. In Nielsen Sports, "Unified Measurement: Defining a New Sponsorship Currency," June 1, 2017.

4. Ibid.

5. See Chapter 4.

6. In Billy Witz, "Yankees' Wins Do Not Extend to Ticket Sales," *New York Times,* May 26, 2017.

7. In Fox Sports Press Pass, "World Series Game 7 Averaged over 40 Million Viewers," Nov. 3, 2016 (W).

8. Nielsen Sports, analysis prepared for author, July 2016.

9. Interview with the author.

10. Nielsen analysis prepared for author, July 2016.

11. *The 2015 Year in Sports Media Report,* Nielsen Sports, Feb. 3, 2016.

12. In Jorge Encines, "How Latinos Are Helping M.L.B. Learn Spanish," NPR, March 28. 2017.

13. Evan Lenow, "Baseball and the State of the American Family," *Canon and Culture,* May 18, 2015.

14. *Real Sports with Bryant Gumbel,* HBO, April 22, 2015.

15. Derrick Williams, "The Williams Sisters Are Examples of Hope for Americans Who Live in Fear," *The Guardian,* Jan. 29, 2017.

16. Interview with the author.

17. Marc Armour and Daniel L. Levitt, "Baseball Demographics, 1947–2016," Society for American Baseball Research (W).

18. Branson Wright, "A Team-by-Team List of African-American M.L.B. Players," The Undefeated, April 14, 2017 (W).

19. *Real Sports* interview.

20. Interview with the author.

21. In Drew Harwell, "Women Are Pro Football's Most Important Demographic. Will They Forgive the N.F.L.?" *Washington Post,* Sept. 12, 2014.

22. In Ron Clements, "Donald Trump Clearly Doesn't Know What Concussions Are as He Mocks N.F.L.," *Sporting News,* Oct. 12, 2016 (W).

23. Roger Angell, "Sharing the Beat," in *Late Innings* (New York, 1982), p. 118.

24. Kristie Ackert, "Proud to Stand with Claire Smith as Pioneering Baseball Writer Earns Her Place in the Hall of Fame," *New York Daily News,* Dec. 7, 2016.

25. Ibid.

26. In Angell, "Sharing the Beat," p. 150.

27. Doug Glanville, "Who Gets to Call the Game?" *New York Times,* July 29, 2017.

28. Flip Bondy, "Statistical Imbalance: Membership Lacks Youth," *New York Times,* July 1, 2017.

29. Quoted in Larry Tye, *Satchel: The Life and Times of an American Legend* (New York, 2010), p. 297.

1. Quoted in Thomas Boswell, "Always Leave 'Em Laughing," *How Life Imitates the World Series* (New York, 1982), p. 289.

2. Ibid., p. 283.

3. Quoted in Mike Lupica, "His Legacy Is a Big, Unfillable Void," *Shooting from the Lip* (Chicago, 1986), p. 278.

4. Stephen Miller, *Conversation: A History of a Declining Art* (New Haven), 2006.

5. In Tyler Kepner, "Commissioner Chides Union for Resisting Changes," *New York Times,* Feb. 22, 2017.

6. Quoted in Bob Nightengale, "M.L.B. Union Chief Tony Clark: Rule Changes Unlikely, Yankees' Levine 'Unprofessional,'" *USA Today,* Feb. 10, 2017.

7. Jesse Spector, "Major League Baseball Has a Poor Understanding of 'Time is Money,'" *Dealbreaker,* Feb. 13, 2017 (W).

8. Tom Gatto, "M.L.B. Gets It Wrong Again with Change to Intentional Walk Rule," *Sporting News,* Feb. 22, 2017.

9. George Vecsey, "Fixing What Ain't Broke? That's Ruinous," *New York Times,* February 11, 2017.

10. Quoted in Bob Nightengale, "Like It or Not, M.L.B. to Implement Pitch Clock in 2018," *USA Today,* July 11, 2017.

11. Rob Arthur, "Baseball's Biggest Games Are Taking Forever," www.fivethirtyeight.com (W).

12. Ibid.

13. Quoted in Jerry Izenberg, *The Greatest Game Ever Played* (New York, 1987), p. 50.

14. Ibid.

15. Philip Roth, *Patrimony* (New York, 1991), pp. 141–42.

16. "Baseball's Too Slow. Here's How to Fix It," *New York Times,* March 2, 2017.

17. Quoted in Jeff Passan, "M.L.B. Plans to Test New Extra-Innings Rule in Rookie Ball, with Joe Torre's Approval," Yahoo Sports, Feb. 6, 2017 (W).

18. Dave Sheinin, "Baseball Has Pace-of-Play Problems; Extra Innings Aren't One of Them," *Washington Post,* Feb. 9, 2017.

19. One of the best books on the strike was written by William J. Gould IV, former head of the National Labor Relations Board. In *Bargaining with Baseball: Labor Relations in an Age of Prosperous Turmoil* (Jefferson, N.C., 2011), Gould traces the long-term impact of the dispute.

20. Kurt Badenhausen, "How M.L.B. Roared Back after 1994 Strike, with Revenue Up 400%," *Forbes,* April 11, 2014.

21. Interview with the author.

22. "Unified Measurement: Defining a New Sponsorship Currency," Nielsen Sports, June 1, 2017 (W).

FIVE: THE "NATIONAL PASTIME" AND THE NATIONAL CULTURE OF DISTRACTION

1. "Kids Increasingly Stare at Glowing Screens, Study Finds," National Public Radio, Oct. 25, 2011 (W).

2. Entertainment Software Association, Jan. 19, 2017 (W).

3. Quoted in Michael S. Rosenwald, "Youth Sports Participation Is Up Slightly, but Many Kids Are Still Left Behind," *Washington Post,* May 17, 2016.

4. "Children and Electronic Media: How Much Is Too Much?" American Psychological Association, "In the Public Interest" newsletter, June 2015 (W).

5. "Unified Measurement," Nielsen Sports, June 1, 2017.

6. "Amanda Lenhart, "Teens, Social Media, and Technology: Overview 2015," Pew Research Center, April 9, 2015.

7. "Radio in the 1930s," *History Detectives,* Public Broadcasting Service (W).

8. Interview with the author.

9. "Industry Demographics," Fantasy Sports Trade Association, June 6, 2017.

10. Quoted in Nadia Kounang, CNN, "The Time-Sucking, Dopamine-Boosting Science of Fantasy Baseball," March 18, 2016.

11. Brent Schrotenboer, "Leagues See Real Benefits in Fantasy Sports," *USA Today,* Jan. 1, 2015.

12. In Joe Drape, "Win for DraftKings and FanDuel Opens Door for Sports Betting in New York," *New York Times,* Aug. 3, 2016.

13. Ibid.

14. Renee Miller, "M.L.B. Daily Games Strategy: Comparative Lessons," Oct. 8, 2014, www.rotowire.com (W).

15. In Amiri Tulloch, "M.L.B. Commissioner Rob Manfred's Plan to Grow Baseball, One Kid at a Time," Sports Illustrated Kids, www.sikids.com., March 30, 2015 (W).

16. "2016 Shape of the Nation," Shape America, www.shapeamerica.org, April 4, 2016 (W).

17. In Shehan Jeyarajah, "M.L.B. Kicks Off Play Ball Youth Baseball Initiative," Sports Illustrated Kids, www.sikids.com., June 19, 2015 (W).

18. "State of Play: 2016," Project Play, Aspen Institute, June 22, 2016. See also Brian Costa, "Why Children Are Abandoning Baseball," *Wall Street Journal,* May 20, 2015; Rosenwald, "Youth Participation in Sports"; and Susan Jacoby, "Baseball and Its Aging Fans, *Wall Street Journal,* August 18, 2016.

1. Terry Bluett, "Baseball and the Civil War," Pennsylvania Civil War Trails, www.pacivilwartrails.com (W).

2. Debbie Schaefer-Jacobs, "Civil War Baseball," Smithsonian, National Museum of American History, Kenneth E. Behring Center, Aug. 2, 2012, http://americanhistory.si.edu (W).

3. Ibid.

4. Quoted in Anson, "Cap: Baseball Hall of Fame," http://baseball hall.org/hof/anson-cap.

5. Joe Vasile, "Black Players in Organized White Baseball in the Pre-integration Era," *Beyond the Box Score,* Feb. 1, 1915 (W.)

6. Philip Roth, "My Baseball Years," *Reading Myself and Others* (New York, 1985), p. 237.

7. Kay Lazar, "Day after Jones Incident, Red Sox Eject, Ban Fan over Slur," *Boston Globe,* May 4, 2017.

8. Franklin D. Roosevelt to Kenesaw Mountain Landis, Jan. 15, 1942. The original of the letter is located in the Baseball Hall of Fame in Cooperstown, N.Y. A carbon is kept in the Franklin D. Roosevelt Library in Hyde Park, N.Y.

9. Gerald Bazer and Steven Culbertson, "When FDR Said 'Play Ball': President Called Baseball a Wartime Morale Booster," *National Archives,* Spring 2002, vol. 34, no. 1.

10. Richard Goldstein, *Spartan Seasons: How Baseball Survived the Second World War* (New York, 1980), pp. 41–42, cited ibid.

11. Jeff Obermeyer, *Baseball and the Bottom Line in World War II: Gunning for Profits on the Home Front* (Jefferson, N.C., 2013), p. 68.

12. J. G. Taylor Spink, "It's Not the Same Game in Japan, *Sporting News,* Dec. 18, 1941.

13. Quoted in Larry Tye, "After a Lot of Errors, the Hall of Fame's Home Run," *Los Angeles Times,* July 24, 2009.

14. "If You Punch Us, We Punch Back," June 14, 2017, www.cnn
.com (W).

15. The video, and Thompson's introduction, are available on You-
Tube at many Web sites.

16. Michael L. Butterworth, *Baseball and Rhetorics of Purity: The National Pastime and American Identity during the War on Terror* (Tuscaloosa, Ala., 2010), p. 5.

17. Quoted in Lawrence Ritter, *The Glory of Their Times: The Story
of the Early Days of Baseball Told by the Men Who Played It* (New York,
1985), p. 48.

selected bibliography

Aaron, Hank, with Lonnie Wheeler. *I Had a Hammer: The Hank Aaron Story.* New York: Harper Collins, 1991.

Angell, Roger. *Five Seasons: A Baseball Companion.* New York: Simon and Schuster, 1977.

———. *Late Innings: A Baseball Companion.* New York: Simon and Schuster, 1982.

———. *Season Ticket: A Baseball Companion.* Boston: Houghton Mifflin, 1988.

Boswell, Thomas. *How Life Imitates the World Series: An Inquiry into the Game.* New York: Doubleday, 1982.

———. *Why Time Begins on Opening Day.* New York: Viking Penguin, 1985.

Butterworth, Michael L. *Baseball and Rhetorics of Purity: The National Pastime and American Identity during the War on Terror.* Tuscaloosa: University of Alabama Press, 2010.

Carkeet, David. *The Greatest Slump of All Time.* New York: Harper and Row, 1980.

Carter, Gary, and John Hough, Jr. *A Dream Season.* New York: Harcourt Brace Jovanovich, 1988.

Creamer, Robert W. *Babe: The Legend Comes to Life.* New York: Penguin, 1983.

Einstein, Charles. *Willie's Time: A Memoir.* New York: Lippincott, 1979.

————, ed. *The Baseball Reader.* New York: McGraw-Hill, 1983.

Furst, R. Terry. *Early Baseball and the Sporting Press.* Jefferson, N.C.: McFarland, 2014.

Giamatti, A. Bartlett. *A Great and Glorious Game: Baseball Writings of A. Bartlett Giamatti,* ed. Kenneth S. Robson. Chapel Hill, N.C.: Algonquin, 1998.

Goodwin, Doris Kearns. *Wait till Next Year: A Memoir.* New York: Touchstone, 1997.

Gould, Bill, IV. *Bargaining with Baseball: Labor Relations in an Era of Prosperous Turmoil.* Jefferson, N.C.: McFarland, 2011.

Hall, Donald. *Fathers Playing Catch with Sons: Essays on Sport (Mostly Baseball).* San Francisco: North Point, 1985.

Hernandez, Keith, and Mike Bryan. *If at First . . .: A Season with the Mets.* New York: Viking Penguin, 1987.

Holtzman, Jerome, ed. *Fielder's Choice: An Anthology of Baseball Fiction.* New York: Harcourt Brace Jovanovich, 1979.

Hye, Allen E. *Religion in Modern Baseball Fiction.* Macon, Ga.: Mercer University Press, 2004.

Izenberg, Jerry. *The Greatest Game Ever Played.* New York: Henry Holt, 1987.

James, Bill. *The Bill James Historical Baseball Abstract.* New York: Villard, 1988.

Kahn, Roger. *The Boys of Summer.* New York: New American Library, 1973.

Kinsella, W. P. *Shoeless Joe.* Boston: Houghton Mifflin, 1982.

Klein, Alan. *Dominican Baseball: New Pride, Old Prejudice.* Philadelphia: Temple University Press, 2014.

Lupica, Mike. *Shooting from the Lip*. Chicago: Bonus, 1988.

Malamud, Bernard. *The Natural*. New York: Harcourt, Brace, 1952.

McNeil, William F. *The Evolution of Pitching in Major League Baseball*. Jefferson, N.C.: McFarland, 2006.

Nash, Bruce, and Allan Zullo, eds. *The Baseball Hall of Shame 2*. New York: Pocket Books, 1986.

Obermeyer, Jeff. *Baseball and the Bottom Line in World War II: Gunning for Profits on the Home Front*. Jefferson, N.C.: McFarland, 2013.

Okrent, Daniel. *Nine Innings: The Anatomy of Baseball as Seen Through the Playing of a Single Game*. Boston: Houghton Mifflin, 1994.

———. *The Ultimate Baseball Book*. Boston: Houghton Mifflin, 1991.

Ritter, Lawrence. *The Glory of Their Times: The Story of the Early Days of Baseball as Told by the Men Who Played It*. New York: Vintage, 1985.

Roth, Philip. *The Great American Novel*. New York: Holt, Rinehart and Winston, 1973.

———. *Patrimony*. New York: Simon and Schuster, 1991.

———. *Reading Myself and Others*. Penguin, 1985.

Solderholm-Difatte, Bryan. *The Golden Era of Major League Baseball: A Time of Transition and Integration*. New York: Rowman and Littlefield, 2015.

Spalding, Albert G. *America's National Game: Historic Facts Concerning the Beginning, Evolution, Popularity and Development of Base Ball*. New York: American Sports Publishing, 1911; rpt. Lincoln: University of Nebraska Press, 1992.

Thorn, John, and James Stevenson, eds. *The Armchair Book of Baseball*. New York: Charles Scribner's Sons, 1985.

Turkle, Sherry. *Life on the Screen: Identity in the Age of the Internet*. New York: Simon and Schuster, 1995.

Tye, Larry. *Satchel: The Life and Times of an American Legend*. New York: Random House, 2010.

Tygiel, Jules. *Past Time: Baseball as History.* New York: Oxford University Press, 2000.

Veeck, Bill, with Ed Linn. *Veeck—As in Wreck: The Autobiography of Bill Veeck.* New York: Putnam, 1962.

acknowledgments

First, I wish to thank Sal Tuzzeo and his team of statisticians at Nielsen Sports for breaking out numbers from Nielsen's 2014, 2015, and 2016 year-end sports reviews to give me greater insight into the demographics of baseball fans who watch the game on television and mobile devices. The volume of statistics is staggering, and the Nielsen staff's cooperation was indispensable to me.

Many who work in the business of baseball provided me with a different kind of help by arranging interviews—sometimes during the baseball season itself, when everyone involved with the game is overwhelmed by such requests. Pat Courtney, assistant to the commissioner of Major League Baseball, and Greg Bouris, director of communications for the Major League Baseball Players Association, were especially helpful.

Alex Lee, a political scientist with extensive knowledge about the statistics and politics of baseball, provided me with a wealth of ideas about the attitudes of various generations toward the game.

This is the sixth book I have written and researched in the Frederick Lewis Allen Room of that great institution, the New York Public Library. I owe special thanks to Carolyn Broomhead and Melanie Locay, who oversaw the research rooms for writers while I was working on this book.

At Yale University Press, I owe so much to so many people. First, the Press's director, John Donatich, took the time, when he was under a great deal of pressure, to read every word of *Why Baseball Matters* and make several invaluable suggestions. Dan Heaton edited the manuscript meticulously, and—I hate to admit this—knows more about baseball than I have forgotten. Sonia Shannon designed the perfect jacket. Danielle D'Orlando, acquisitions department manager, seemed to do just about everything to keep production moving smoothly.

My friends Hank Burchard and Mark Lee, who are not ardent baseball fans, nevertheless listened to me talk endlessly about this book. They listened, I should emphasize, when some other nonbaseball friends would have hung up on me.

index

Susan Jacoby, who began her writing career as a reporter for the *Washington Post,* is the author of twelve books, including the *New York Times* best seller *The Age of American Unreason* (2008); *Freethinkers: A History of American Secularism; The Great Agnostic: Robert Ingersoll and American Freethought* (2013); and *Strange Gods: A Secular History of Conversion.*

Jacoby has been a contributor to a wide range of periodicals and newspapers for more than thirty-five years, on topics including secularism, baseball, aging, law, medicine, women's rights, and political dissent in the Soviet Union and post-Soviet Russia. Her articles and essays have appeared in the *New York Times,* the *Washington Post,* the *Los Angeles Times,* the *Wall Street Journal,* the *American Prospect,* the *Daily Beast,* and the *Nation,* among other publications. They have been reprinted in numerous anthologies of columns and magazine articles.

Jacoby has been the recipient of many grants and awards, from the Guggenheim, Rockefeller, and Ford Foundations, as well as the National Endowment for the Humanities. In 2001, she was named a fellow at the Dorothy and Lewis B. Cullman Center for Scholars and Writers at the New York Public Library.

Susan Jacoby lives in New York City.

Featuring intriguing pairings of authors and subjects, each volume in the **Why X Matters** series presents a concise argument for the continuing relevance of an important idea.